# MORE THAN THIS

Your Heroic Quest to Find

Inspiration, **Intent**, **Impact** and **Insight**

in a Broken World

Rebecca Elvy

Rebecca Elvy Publishing

First Published 2018 by Rebecca Elvy Publishing, Wellington

www.rebeccaelvy.com

ISBN 978-0-473-44217-0

For Logan.

For a better world for all of our children.

Cover design: Sara Mason

Contents ❧

Introduction 🦋

When Your 'Why' Makes You Cry

"If there is dissatisfaction with the status quo, good. If there is ferment, so much the better. If there is restlessness, I am pleased. Then let there be ideas, and hard thought, and hard work. If man feels small, let man make himself bigger." Hubert H. Humphrey

On 3 August 2007 a three year old girl died in Starship Children's Hospital after 13 days on life support. Her brain damage was so severe that she couldn't breathe without the machines. The injuries she sustained over several weeks leading up to her admission to hospital make for chilling reading. She was kicked, dropped, hit. She was folded into a sofa and sat on. She was put on a rotary clothesline and spun so fast she flew off. She was crammed into a clothes drier that was turned on for 30 minutes. On high.

And the doctors who cared for her upon her admission said that she would have survived had she been taken to hospital immediately. Instead, her 35 year old mother went to a 21st birthday party for five days and left her in the care of the monsters who had inflicted this despicable violence in the first place. Her 19 year old partner and his mates.

They thought she was ugly.

Her name was Nia Glassie.

Eight years later, on 10 August 2015, Moko Rangitoheriri died following abuses that the coroner said made what happened to Nia seem like "kindergarten". He was kicked, thrown, dropped, bitten and stomped on over the course of several weeks. I cannot write the injuries he sustained. Or the terrors inflicted upon him in his last days alive.

His 'carers' said he was "taking them for granted".

He, too, was three years old.

Both of these cases took place in New Zealand. A small country with a population of about four million. They outraged a nation. The trials and sentencing of the accused took centre stage on the nightly news. In both cases there were other children who witnessed the atrocities – in some cases being forced to participate.

And although there was outrage, and although policy changes were made to place greater emphasis on protection of vulnerable children, and although processes were improved to ensure social service agencies worked more closely together, we still don't know how to *prevent* such tragedies from occurring.

I'm not sharing these stories with you to be sensationalist. Or to in any way exploit[*] what happened to these two beautiful children at the hands of the adults who were supposed to be taking care of them. This book is part of my attempt to make their lives, and the lives of others who have died in senseless ways, mean something. I won't make reference to these two cases again in this book – so if this upset you, I have two things to say. Good, it should. And, don't worry – this isn't a book full of harrowing stories.

A good friend said to me recently "if your why doesn't make you cry, you haven't found your why".

This.

This is what makes me cry.

This is a book for people who think that crying is not enough. Not nearly enough. This is a book for people who see things like this in the world and want to do more than cry. This is a book for people who want to *do something*. This is a book for people who feel compelled to act but don't know where to start.

This is a book for people who *know* they should do something, but don't believe that they are big enough, or clever enough, or qualified enough.

For people who worry that one person can't make a difference.

---

[*] Ideally, I would have obtained permission from Nia and Moko's families before including their names in this book. I didn't, because I was also concerned that they are already in enough pain. If anyone from their families wants to reach out to me, my contact information is included in this book.

To you I say stop thinking that way. It's the only thing that ever has.

I grew up believing my brain was my greatest asset. I wasn't particularly pretty, rich or athletic. If I was going to make it in the world, it would be me and my brain.

And it's a pretty good brain. I aced the Mensa entrance exam with a score in the 99th percentile (you only need 98 to get in). I have a very good memory – which was a huge help learning languages and music, and even entry level math. I thought, for a while that I might be a brain surgeon, brains fascinated me so much. Blood on the other hand, not so much… so I gave that one away well before I went to high school! I see patterns and solve problems naturally. I'm very fond of my brain. I have always felt that I am obliged to find ways to put it to good use!

In spring 2005, I was leaving my cheap, student flat with my partner Dale, when I slipped down an external flight of stairs. I landed on my backside. It hurt, a lot. I was winded and walked a bit funny for quite a few days afterwards.

A few weeks later, though, I started noticing that my feet tingled when I tilted my head forward. It was very unpleasant and disconcerting. It went on for a couple of weeks, and I eventually went to my doctor, assuming I had a pinched nerve.

My GP though, was less convinced about my diagnosis. She referred me for blood tests and sent me on my way.

A few days later, she rang me to say she didn't think there was any point doing X-rays, that she was going to refer me to a specialist. Also, that my blood tests showed I had very low Vitamin B12 levels, but no indications of pernicious anaemia.

"Do you huff nitrous oxide or are you vegan?" she asked casually.

"Um, no"?

Fast forward quite a few months and my appointment at outpatient neurology came around. I went by myself. To be honest, it never occurred to me that I should take someone with me. I mean, the tingling had gone away! I was fit, healthy, young…

I remember sitting in the waiting room for what seemed like forever, reading the posters on the wall. Support groups for people with Parkinson's Disease, Multiple Sclerosis, Dementia, Alzheimer's, brain tumours, stroke…

I wasn't worried when I arrived, but by the time my name was called out, I was terrified.

I can't remember much about the actual consultation at all. There was a medical student present – I know I gave permission for that. I had to do a bunch of weird things like stand on one foot with my eyes closed, finding the tip of my nose with my finger without looking, and I had pins stuck in the soles of my feet. It wasn't invasive, but it was thorough. To be honest, the conversation between the specialist and the student was the worst part. It was full of medical terms, jargon, technical language. I had no idea what they were talking about. And it just compounded my fear.

By the end of the appointment I was none the wiser, but I was definitely 100 per cent more afraid.

I left to catch the bus home by myself. Dale wasn't home. At a bit of a loose end, and trying desperately to replay the consultation in my mind, I remembered that I'd heard some sort of diagnostic term towards the end of the discussion. But I hadn't written it down. I hadn't even asked them to repeat it.

I was scared and felt helpless.

Then I had an idea... Google.

I described the foot tingling sensation and hit search.

After multiple pages of traumatising search results, I found a term that sounded familiar. Lhermitt's Sign: an electric shock-like sensation that occurs on flexion of the neck. This sensation radiates down the spine, often into the legs, arms, and sometimes to the trunk. A classic symptom of Multiple Sclerosis. I was 26 years old.

A few days later I received a letter from the hospital confirming an appointment at radiology for an MRI. I did the MRI by myself too, but I knew enough now to take Dale with me when I got the results.

Sure enough, there on the lightbox was an image of my brain with five 'pea-sized' white spots.

The neurologist said "If you're planning to have a family you should start soon. You probably won't be able to walk by the time you're fifty. If you have any more symptoms you should make an appointment with your GP."

To be officially diagnosed with MS, you need to have *multiple* episodes. It's in the name! But the almost-diagnosis didn't sit well with me.

Of course, I was worried – scared even. I was young. I loved my brain! Why was this happening to me? What did it all mean? Would it be fast or slow? How much time did I have?

After a few months of mostly forgetting, but sometimes devastatingly remembering the looming reality, I decided two things:

- I didn't have MS, it must be something else; and
- If I *did* have MS, I was gonna get a wriggle on and get some serious career runs on the board while I still could…

I became hyper-aware of every peculiar sensation in my body. Every set of pins and needles, every tingle, every numbness. I did have other symptoms… Optic neuritis (a lesion on my optic nerve) which made it hurt to move my eyeball and made my vision go dim and greyish in one eye. A strange facial tingling that made me feel like my speech wasn't forming properly and slowed down my talking. Tingles running outwards and down my arms. Trouble typing…

But with my decisions (one of which – at times – felt a bit unrealistic) I determined not to return to my GP. Instead, I focused on where I wanted to get to in my life – the things I was going to accomplish, the lifestyle I wanted to live, the adventures I wanted to have – and I started learning everything I could about the disease.

I attended seminars and conferences, I read books, I scoured the internet. I read more books. I started taking supplements of Vitamin B12 and Vitamin D. I absorbed everything I could possibly find about what is (and isn't) known about the causes of MS.

At the same time, I enrolled in and completed a Master's Degree. Dale and I started a business. I got a new and more senior job. Most of the time, I was doing all three of these things at once!

I'm not going to bore you with all the gory details… (actually gory would be interesting – there was a great deal of tedium!) but fast-forward 12 years and…

- I have four degrees (a Bachelors, a Masters, a Graduate Diploma and a Post-Graduate Diploma)
- I am Chief Executive of a medium-sized charity
- I have a thriving coaching and leadership development practice
- I have a four-year-old son and a husband (yes, Dale who was there when I fell down the stairs, and came with me for the MRI results!)

… And I've been symptom free for 10 years.

What I've learned along the way is that most people are wasting their lives on stuff that doesn't matter because they don't know any different.

I want to help you wake up from that. To stop waiting and start living. Because you can. I want you to live on purpose and be the CEO of you. And I believe that if enough people do this, phenomenal things will happen. The world will literally be a better place.

So I want to teach you what I've learned about kick-starting your life. I want to give you the tools you'll need to build and sustain massive momentum. And I want to help you create and achieve the kind of impact that you've always dreamed you'd make – irrespective of whether you're the executive assistant or the chief executive.

I've also noticed that most people constrain what they are capable of based on what they see happening around them. Most people are **resigned**. They are resigned to the fact that politicians are corrupt and aren't trying to fix the problems occurring in the country. They are resigned to the fact that climate change is inevitable and cannot be influenced by human effort. They are resigned to the fact that some people are just bad, and will do bad things no matter what happens. They are resigned to the fact that some people have to sweep the streets and empty the rubbish bins and mop the floors. They are resigned to the fact that there are so many problems in the world that there's no point trying to do anything about it.

When did you give up on your dreams? And what brought it about? And more importantly, how do you feel about it now? Are you relieved? Does it remove the pressure? Or is there just a little bit of you that resents the fact that you've 'settled' for less?

We talk about people leading their lives, but we dismiss what leadership means in this context. It's almost like 'leading a life' is some lesser form of leadership – or not leadership at all.

I want you to change that thinking right now.

You are the chief executive of you. Nobody else can hold that role. And you shouldn't *let* anybody else hold that role.

Leadership is not a job. It's something everybody does every day. The question is not whether you lead – but why, how and for what purpose?

We live in interesting times. A quick scan of the world headlines and it's plain to see that chasms are opening up within society that seem unfathomably deep and unbridgeable... Previously impenetrable boundaries are being crossed with ease...

Simple slogans are winning out over facts with alarming regularity... Leadership matters in many ways. It matters for the ability to see a better future, and to share that vision with people. It matters for the ability to nurture and grow others. It matters for the ability to foster innovation and growth. It matters for the ability to inspire others to be the best versions of themselves.

But leadership matters most when it overcomes the temptation to reduce complicated things to catchy slogans, and when it enables people to understand and engage with wicked problems in new and creative ways.

When I look at the world we live in, it is clear to me that people exactly like you need to step up and lead. Now I don't (just) mean positional leadership – like managers and CEOs. I mean leaders in the broadest sense – leaders of movements, leaders of people, leaders of ideas, leaders of change, leaders of impactful lives.

There are a multitude of problems crying out for solutions: from climate change, to famine, to civil war, to inequality, to human rights abuses, to corruption, to nuclear arms proliferation, to drought, to child abuse...

If you have ever looked at these problems – or problems like them – and thought "I wish I could do something about that", then this book is for you. This book will help you find the inspiration to reach out and tackle that big (or modest or small) problem you care about. Then it will help you turn that inspiration into actual intent. A decision to do something. Then it will give you the tools and skills to impact change in the world. Not just because you can, but because you must. You, your family, your friends and the world, need you to.

Great leaders revel in the challenge of reconciling two apparently irreconcilable ideas, because they know that is where the creativity happens.

Great leaders embrace the grey areas between polar opposites, because they know life is seldom black and white.

Great leaders explore the murky complexities of important issues, because they know the devil can be in the detail.

Great leaders critically examine slogans and by-lines to see whether they pass the sniff-test, because they know that sales-pitches leave out the most important features in a bid to appeal to our emotions.

Great leaders recognise that by simplifying things to their barest essentials, we lose the essence of what made them important in the first place.

Leadership matters because sometimes long-held conventions are no longer sufficient to protect our institutions and systems from tearing themselves apart.

Please don't misunderstand me. I'm not saying complexity is good and simplicity is bad – I'm saying it's never that simple.

I fundamentally believe that all people have the potential within them to achieve greatness.

There are plenty of things in the world to worry about – and some of them you can do something about. Actually many of them. But only if you're prepared to *not* do something else.

For the rest, have hope and optimism in your fellow human beings, and get on with making the very best of the cards you have been dealt. Within that hand lies the power to make a real difference – to your life, to the lives of your family and friends, and to the lives of millions of people all around the world.

Let's get inspired, set our intention, and impact the world for the better!

Who Is This Book For?

"Learning is the beginning of wealth. Learning is the beginning of health. Learning is the beginning of

spirituality. Searching and learning is where the miracle process all begins." Jim Rohn

Before we get underway, it's worth pausing for a minute to consider who this book is for.

While it is true that there is no perfect person who'll find this book meaningful – or more useful, I can say that there are three characteristics that you need to have if you want to implement what this book outlines.

Future Orientation

In their book *The Time Paradox: The New Psychology of Time*, Philip Zimbardo (instigator of the infamous Stanford prison experiments) and John Boyd set out a number of psychological concepts about the way the human brain processes time – or at least, how we perceive time.

In it, they also outline their research on *Time Perspectives*. They identified that people can be categorised as having a time profile, based on their answers to a short questionnaire. They also identify what they consider to be the optimal time profile based on demonstrated life outcomes.

The six possible time perspectives[*] are:

---

[*] If you're curious, you can take their survey online at http://www.thetimeparadox.com/zimbardo-time-perspective-inventory/ and determine for yourself which of these most accurately describes you. It's also important to note that your time perspective does change over your lifetime.

- Past-negative
- Past-positive
- Present-fatalistic
- Present-hedonistic
- Future
- Transcendental-future

Suffice to say, to really put the lessons in this book to best use, you need a healthy dose of 'future'. Also, a small amount of past-negative.

Personally, I'm not religious, so I cannot easily comment on the value of transcendental-future for engaging with the lessons in this book, but it seems plausible to me that transcendental-future may be equally valuable with 'Future'. I'll let you decide when you complete the inventory.

Why this focus on time?

Well this book is all about improving things. Making a better future through your own impact. If you predominantly view the world as entirely about living in the moment and going with the flow (Present-hedonistic) or that there's no point trying because it won't make any difference (Present-fatalistic) you're going to find it pretty difficult to get motivated to change the world!

Seeing time as a flow that you can influence is a really important part of this journey.

I should note though, that even if you do complete the inventory and discover that your time perspective doesn't exactly match what

I've suggested here, it's worth getting a copy of the book. In it, Zimbardo and Boyd also explain why time perspectives matter generally, and how to influence your time perspective. There is an entire chapter dedicated to ways you can tweak or adjust your own time perspective to bring it into line with something that will serve you better.

I personally am biased towards the future. I'm constantly searching for things I can do now to impact on the future. Consequently, I completely accept that I'm likely to express a preference for this time perspective, and I probably view it as superior to other perspectives.

This bias may blind me to the ways in which other perspectives can contribute to the world – so don't take my word for it. Complete the inventory and then make your own mind up!

Dissatisfied with the Status Quo

Now you might think that it's rather strange to use the term dissatisfied to describe the person I think can benefit most from this book, but the rationale is simple.

If you think things are already great – even perfect – why would you be motivated to drive change? You probably wouldn't.

Now I also don't mean that you despair over the current state of things (though you may), I simply mean that you look at the world and see things that you recognise could be different... better.

These things might be within your own family, community or workplace, or they may be national or global matters. It could be in the domain of product design (a regular annoyance you or a family member has with a household item that doesn't perform as well as it could) or a global social issue (like inequality). The scale of the issue doesn't matter at all – just that you can see things you'd like to improve.

I refer to this as dissatisfaction. It's a deliberately gentle term. It's not unhappiness or grumpiness (though it may include these). It's just a mild frustration or annoyance. A recognition that things could be better than they are.

Determined to Make a Difference

Now it is possible to be future-oriented and discontented, but still not see it as something you should do anything about. So for the purpose of clarity, let me categorically state that this book is for people who want to make a difference.

You might not know how, or even why, when or where, but that doesn't matter, provided you'd like to figure it out and give it a go.

I suspect you already have this though, or you probably wouldn't have picked up this book and read this far!

Who Isn't This Book For?

It should be said that there are also some people for whom this book is unlikely to be of any use at all. If you fall into one or more of these categories, don't buy it. I don't want you to waste your time.

Victim Mindset

"To complain is always nonacceptance of what is. It invariably carries an unconscious negative charge. When you complain, you make yourself into a victim.

18

When you speak out, you are in your power. So change the situation by taking action or by speaking out if necessary or possible; leave the situation or accept it. All else is madness." Eckhart Tolle

In psychology, this is referred to as having an external locus of control. In other words, you don't see yourself as being in control of what happens to you or your responses to those things, you see the world as happening to you, and consequently, you don't feel like you have any control.

I've always been a very positive person. I refer to myself as an optimist. I enjoy finding the silver lining in every cloud. I've been called Pollyanna.

And when I worked through the Simon Sinek *Find Your Why* process with somebody else, I was surprised to see how many of the formative life experiences that I remembered could be seen as quite negative situations. My parents' divorce, my father's anger, my mum's inconsistency, my father's absence post-divorce, our lack of resources, having to travel 16 kilometres by bicycle to catch the bus to travel 40 kilometres to get to school… and then having to get home again afterwards…

But even though these circumstances were no doubt challenging at the time, I choose to see them as pivotal and important moments in my life. Moments that made me who I am today. I'm pretty sure that I would not be as resilient and self-reliant and successful as I am if I hadn't had those experiences to learn from. I'm certain I wouldn't be nearly as good a wife and mother without the negative experiences to learn what *not* to do.

So what is the difference between people like this and people who think the sky is falling? It's all about how they choose to relate to those experiences. Optimists choose to see negative events and setbacks as an opportunity to test themselves, to push their limits, and to learn something new.

And do you know what the funny thing is? When you look for these opportunities, you *always* find them. My deep suspicion is that they were always there, but not everybody looks... and so not everybody finds.[*]

I've found no evidence that there is a law-of-attraction, and that the universe is vibrating just for you... but I have seen and experienced concrete evidence that what you look for in the world determines what you find in the world. So if you think that the world just 'happens' to you, and that you have no control over things, that's exactly how you will experience the world. Those exact same experiences, when they 'happen' to someone who is looking for

---

[*] There is actually lab-based scientific evidence that optimists are 'luckier' than pessimists. In a study conducted by Professor Richard Wiseman, subjects were put into one of two categories based on their self-reported levels of optimism or pessimism, and then asked to look through a newspaper, counting the number of photographs. The people who identified as unlucky took, on average, two minutes to count all the photographs. The people who saw themselves as lucky took just a few seconds. Why? Because a few pages in there was a half-page advert with the words: "Stop counting. There are 43 photographs in this newspaper." The unlucky people didn't see it – and went on counting manually. After a while, Wiseman added another page to the newspaper – another half page advert that said "Stop counting, tell the experimenter you have seen this and win £150." They missed this too.

opportunities to grow and learn, become growth and learning opportunities.

Contented

Perhaps ironically, the near opposite is true too.

If you think the world is perfect already, there's a fairly high chance that your level of desire to change it will be too low to sustain the type of effort and motivation that I'm going to outline in this book.

If the world is great, why get off the couch? If the world is great, why try and change it?

Please don't be confused, I'm not suggesting that you shouldn't reflect on what you have achieved, and be grateful for the many wonderful things around you. I'm simply saying if there is nothing in the world you think needs to change, then thanks for reading this far, but you should probably pass this on to a slightly less contented friend…

Or you could try experimenting with a different mindset. Even in a perfect world, there must be something you could imagine being better?

Fear of Change

> *"If you don't like something, change it. If you can't change it, change your attitude." Maya Angelou*

Yes, change is scary. And actually your brain is biologically driven to avoid change – irrespective of whether it is change created by you or happening around you.

When our prehistoric ancestors roamed the planet, change was very slow and unusual. Major innovations were thousands of years apart – not days or even hours.

And, unfortunately for them a major change in the environment was highly likely to spell certain death: a sabre-tooth tiger,[*] a poisonous berry, a natural disaster…

So our brains[†] evolved a mechanism to keep us safe. Thank goodness!

It is our older brain – the limbic system – which predates, evolutionarily speaking, the pre-frontal cortex. The limbic system is where our emotions are processed and our memories formed. It is where the emotional and motivational information that triggers our fight-or-flight response stems from, and ultimately it is in charge of our stress levels.

Today, sabre-tooth-tigers are pretty rare. And I've never spotted one at the office… and yet when our bodies start to notice change and anticipate that something is different or 'off' the fight-or-flight response is exactly what gets triggered.

_____

[*] A word of warning for sabre-tooth tiger fans – they get a bit of a bad rap in this book as a proxy for dangerous predators our brains are pre-conditioned to run away from… Sorry about that. Feel free to substitute it with your own version of a prehistoric predator!

[†] I'm going to talk about brains quite a lot. Understanding what your brain is doing, and why, helps to take some of the mystery out of your own behaviour. I'll also refer to my own brain as a person, from time to time. Because it clearly has its own motivations and drivers – sometimes that are at odds with my own.

In my experience, delivering that major presentation to a key potential client is reasonably unlikely to kill you. There isn't an actual sabre-tooth tiger in the front row eyeing you up as potential lunch… it's just that your brain thinks there is, and wants to make sure you make it through this.

But it is this very disproportional response that can create an unhealthy fear of *all* change. Most of us figure out, at some point, that change is inevitable… we finish school and go to university. We finish university and decide to spend some time travelling before we settle into the 'daily grind'. We move out of our parents' home (hopefully!) and maybe meet someone and start a family. Even in this 'predictable' and relatively conventional life course, there are a multitude of scary and significant changes occurring.

So I'm not suggesting that disliking change *per se* means this book isn't for you, but I am saying if you'd really rather stay at high school where your friends are, or stay at home with your folks because you like the way your dad cooks pancakes, you might have a few other challenges you need to confront first.

How Does It Work?

> *"Ability is what you're capable of doing. Motivation determines what you do. Attitude determines how well you do it." Lou Holtz*

If you've read this far and are still here, I'm going to assume you do see the need for some change – and you're up for the challenge. That you can see things around you in the world that could benefit from a bit of improvement. Great! I'm thrilled to meet you!

The concept of this book is pretty simple, but in my view, powerful. It's based on the idea of a feedback loop.

Now feedback loops are commonly referred to in a business or corporate context – define/plan/measure/review, or some variant on this. It sounds very simple, and in concept it is. But what's hard is actually *doing it*. Many organisations start out with great intentions for using these loops to inform their work, but everyone loses impetus by the time they get to measure and review... By which point they've lost the will to live, or have moved on to the next project.

In my view, this is because the corporate lexicon often doesn't take into account human psychology. There are some people who wake up in the morning going "oooh, measurement! Yippee!". But not many. And typically those people aren't the ones who will come up with your exciting new idea or concept. They probably aren't thinking about all the ways the product or service, or even the world, can be improved.

It's understandable. I get it. But your own life or business doesn't need to be that way.

So instead of 'business terms' this book uses human terms. Personal terms.

Inspiration – Intention – Impact – Insight

It focuses on practical tools to help deliver these things consistently over time.

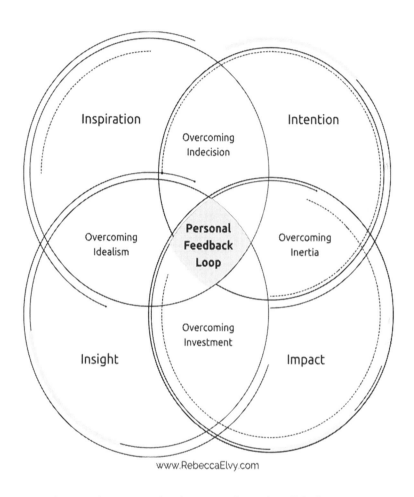

www.RebeccaElvy.com

And most importantly, it recognises that life is messy, and our brains are weird. It recognises that there are a whole bunch of things trying to stop you moving from one stage to the next. It also recognises that most people's lives don't allow them to focus on just one thing at a time, so you can be in different phases of the cycle for different things at the same time. Consequently, between each of the four steps in our "Human Action Feedback Loop" I use the idea of bridging – something that will try to impede your progress that needs to be overcome to be successful. For good measure, I've popped in a couple of important concepts that need to be understood so that you don't get stuck – particularly around intractable problems (or wicked problems as they are referred to in some of the problem-solving literature) and understanding change.

I'm also not interested in reinventing the wheel. So you'll see me refer to other thinkers in this field or related fields to help you along. I've compiled a list of additional reading at the back of the book, but I also want you to be able to work with exactly what's here, so I've included the key bits where I can.

There are a number of resources available on my website www.RebeccaElvy.com/BookResources to assist you in this journey as well, so do head along there and check it out.

Most of all, I want you to enjoy this. I'm not saying it will all be fun – leadership can be challenging and scary and downright hard. But I promise it'll be worth it!

Part One: Inspiration 🦋

1. Introducing Inspiration

"You can't wait for inspiration. You have to go after it with a club." Jack London

Why Does Inspiration Matter?

Human beings are biological creatures that have evolved over time to be as efficient as possible in performing the basic functions of life. This includes, obviously, those that occur within our physiology – respiration, digestion, circulation of blood, renewal of cells, removal of waste products from the blood stream and so on. But it also applies to cognitive and externally physical activities as well.

We prefer to take the easiest path between two points. Sometimes literally.

I studied architecture for a number of years, which, among other things, tends to give you an appreciation for looking at things differently. One of the characteristics of our urban built environments that I often observe is where town planners put pathways – particularly through parks and green spaces. At the planning stage, someone lays out a range of pathways, vistas, experiences as part of an overall design process. It gets built. Then the users of the space – regular people like you and me – gradually reveal the quickest path between two places (where we are and where we are going) by walking that way… irrespective of whether that's where the pathway is or not. Consequently, within a few months of completion, a threadbare track starts to emerge from the perfectly manicured lawn, and ultimately a slightly mucky dirt track marks out the quickest way from point A to point B.

I find these revealed preferences fascinating on a number of fronts. Often (and yes, perhaps it's with the benefit of hindsight) these preferred pathways look obvious. It always makes me wonder how the designer could have overlooked that the entrance to the public car parking building was there and the popular fast-food outlet was here. But also it serves as a reminder that just because you literally lay out a pathway for someone, doesn't mean that they will follow it.

So while it is true that some people are more effective at being efficient with their energy use and time, we generally all have a preference to take the shortest path wherever possible.

The same is true cognitively. Our brains are designed to be as efficient as possible. Mental patterns and through processes that you use frequently – in other words, thoughts that you think often – will physically create changes in your brain so that the neural pathways required to create that thought are more efficient. In other words, the first time you think a thought – learn something or experience something new – that thought might require electrical energy to pass through a rather circuitous route through dozens or even thousands of neurons to reach its destination. But the more often you think that thought or have that experience, the more efficient that pathway will become, until eventually there are a small number of neurons involved, and the connections between them are direct, strong and efficient.

This is exactly why learning something new – like your first day in a new job – can be so mentally draining, and yet after a few weeks or months, it's nothing major.

What does this mean?

Well it means that the things you do often – and the things you think often – are travelling well-trodden and efficient neural pathways, just like the dirt tracks though the park. It also means that doing something new, learning something new, breaking a habit, creating a new habit, all require a tremendous amount of brain power. It's exhausting.

But it gets worse.

You might be wondering why the brain works this way. It doesn't sound very useful. Surely your brain knows that it's better for you in the long run to get off the couch and go for a run? If the new habit you're trying to form is so clearly in your long-term best interests, why would your brain want to get in the way of that?

Hasn't it read the data on increasing rates of obesity, heart disease and type two diabetes?

Well yes, your brain does know these things – intellectually. But for a moment, let's think about why your brain exists and how it evolved.

The architecture of the human brain is basically created from three main structural areas, and while we cannot be entirely certain about how the human brain evolved over time, we can make some educated guesses based on observations of other animals, and an understanding of what each of these brain structures is responsible for doing.

The first part of the brain we'll look at is the brain stem – this sits roughly at the back of your neck and is what your spinal cord connects to. It is responsible for the basic functions that keep you alive. Heartbeat, consciousness, respiration, circulation and the control of body temperature. Essentially, and very importantly, it keeps you alive and gives your body basic instructions about what to do, how often and when.

The second part of the brain to consider is the cerebellum – latin for the word 'little brain'. This structure is, unsurprisingly, more complex, and is primarily responsible for movement.

The third part of your brain is where the experience of being human largely happens – the cerebrum. The human cerebrum is significantly larger (relative to our body size) than any other animal. While it is oversimplified to talk about the structures within this part of the brain as though they are independent of each other (in fact we know that very little happens in the brain that is *entirely* localised to one part of the brain) there are some architectural features of the cerebrum that are worth exploring.

You probably already know that your cerebrum is divided into two hemispheres. This is where the largely disproven concept of 'left-brain/right-brain' thinking stems from. More accurately, this part of your brain has four lobes: the **frontal lobe** – largely responsible for executive function, logic, decision-making, along with our more deliberate and purposeful control of movement, the **parietal lobe** – which includes the areas responsible for our sense of touch (including heat, position, movement), the **temporal lobe** – which includes our auditory functions, and the **occipital lobe** – largely responsible for vision. Why is it wrinkly? To fit in more neurons efficiently. How cool is that!

It's also power hungry – it consumes a massive amount of energy just to keep it running – more when you are thinking about tricky things or big problems. The human neo-cortex is the largest of all animals relative to the overall size of our bodies. And this is a tricky balancing act from a human survival perspective, because having a big neocortex enables us to do some pretty amazing things, but it also creates several major challenges to reproduction – in the form of complications at birth. All that brain makes for a pretty big head!

You may be *less* aware that underneath the blobby-wrinkly grey surface of your brain are a number of other very important brain structures, including the **amygdala** – vital for emotional regulation and motivation, and the **hippocampus** – essential to the creation and recall of memories. This is the part of the brain that is responsible for your fight or flight response. It isn't logical, its emotional. This part of your brain also works to keep you alive, and it does so by manipulating your emotions to alter your physical behaviour.

Because your brain is the largest consumer of energy in your body, consuming 20% of the energy your body needs at rest, it is vital – from a survival standpoint – that energy consumption is as efficient as possible. Which is exactly why your brain – like the general public walking across the grass in the park – must prioritise creating efficient neural pathways for thought processes that occur frequently.

This extreme focus on energy conservation and efficiency going on in your brain is a major reason why it's hard to do something new. It's why you have a 'comfort zone' and it's why remaining in your comfort zone feels 'safe' and moving out of your comfort zone feels incredibly risky – even when intellectually you know that it isn't.

In other words, whenever you want to get off the couch and do something you know you *should* be doing, your brain immediately goes to work to ensure you don't. Especially if you hesitate. Even for just a second. Your brain reads that pause as a sign of danger.

All of this means that you have to find ways to *override* your brain in order to form new habits, learn new skills, and move from your comfort zone into a more developmental space.

This is where inspiration comes in.

While many people describe inspiration as something that is 'out there' in the world, that you find, hopefully, if you're lucky, I need you to think of inspiration a little differently.

I need you to think of inspiration as something that happens inside your head. In effect, while your inspiration may consist of a combination of thoughts and feelings, it is vital to the process we're going to explore in this book, because it becomes a source of metaphorical fuel.

You need to use it as the rocket to get you off the couch when your efficient brain says 'no!'

You need to tap into it when it gets tough and you're wondering whether it's worth it.

You need to draw from it when you are exhausted and would prefer to stop and let somebody else carry the baton.

You need it to create the compulsion to ensure you make the best possible use of your unique talents, skills and perspectives to impact the world with intent.

You need to know what it is, remind yourself of it regularly, and use it to propel you forward into a brave new world – however you define that.

What Is My Inspiration?

My sources of inspiration are many, and varied. As I suspect, are most people's.

For me, it's about breaking the mould, and solving big problems. Things that seem intractable and have defied standard problem-solving approaches.

In some respects, and at its simplest level, my inspiration stems from my dissatisfaction with the status quo. I know the world can be a better place, and I don't accept things have to be the way they are. In addition to that, I'm not interested in fixing symptoms.

I'll give you some examples.

I abhor child abuse. As I'm sure do most people. Yet it happens. A lot more than it should. And in spite of billions of dollars being spent globally to try and curb it, it doesn't seem to be getting better. So clearly the current policy solutions aren't working.

Now one thing I could do is become a foster parent – and absolute kudos to those who do. It's a phenomenal way to help, and for those kids in your care, even though they might not always show it, you are the answer for them.

To me, though, I see that as treating the symptoms. I'd rather try and find a way to stop it from happening in the first place.

Some people would say that's impossible. But I never accept impossibilities. I simply don't agree that anything is impossible, we just haven't figured it out yet – so we have to try harder.

"It always seems impossible until it's done." Nelson Mandela

I am a climate change believer. I have no issue with trusting the science, and I can conceptually understand how even a small amount of human-contribution to global carbon emissions (when weighed against naturally occurring releases of carbon into the atmosphere) can potentially be the straw that breaks the camel's back. The world is full of situations where one little thing pushes a small problem into a big one…

So I do a few things to make sure I manage my own and my family's emissions – but I also know that our contribution is a drop in the bucket.

At this point, you would rightly be saying so what? Lots of people don't like those things. Who likes those things? Surely we can all agree there's bad stuff in the world? Why is that inspiring and what does it have to do with me?

Fair enough. Let's dig deeper…

What Will You Find In This Section?

In this section, we'll introduce two complementary tools to help you find your inspiration. Deceptively simple, but inherently powerful. If you take your time and really engage with the two processes outlined, I just know that you'll be well on your way to connecting with your deeper purpose. Your "why".

A Little Bit About Me

I'm going to share with you a little bit about my story – not because there's anything particularly interesting about me – in fact probably the opposite is true. I'm sharing my story, because I want to use it to show why *your* story is important. My "why" comes from me – my upbringing, my experiences, my memories. Your "why" comes from you. Your upbringing, your experiences, your memories. If you find me boring and choose to skip this bit, that's fine. I promise I won't be offended!

I have a very pronounced memory from early in my childhood – I may have started school, but would be no more than five years old. As the eldest child, I had a number of chores to do around the house every day, one of which was to feed our dog, Kleo. Now we lived on a farm in a small rural community, and Kleo's kennel was a long way (at least to a five-year-old) from our house. My mum would cut the dog-meat, and I would carry it out to Kleo's kennel every night.

This one particular night, I remember distinctly looking up at the sky – it was that in-between period where there's just a couple of stars out, but the sky is a gorgeous tinge of mid-deep blue – the last light still visible, but fading fast. Anyway, I looked up at the stars and I thought to myself "how do I know I'm *me*?" and following closely on the heels of that came "and why am I me and not somebody else?"

Now this thought was deeply engaging to me. My mother will tell you that, like many kids, I asked far too many questions as a child, but this stands out as a defining question for me, and from it stemmed a deep fascination and curiosity about how the brain works – in particular how *my* brain works, but also a willingness to challenge myself to think about really big questions. I was intrigued by the idea that space was infinite. Black holes were terrifying but exciting all at the same time, and this persistent question about how come I ended up in this body, at this time, in this place… it blew my mind.

I know my parents tried to satisfy this curiosity, but we didn't ever have much money, and we didn't live in a city where I could have accessed museums and libraries with resources at the level I was interested in. And just to place my age a little, this was in a long ago time when there was no internet, no smartphones and no

Wikipedia. But we made the most of what we had. My mum in particular encouraged my curiosity, and would try and answer my incessant questions. She also role-modelled – actively – a deep love and value for education. She completed her high school qualifications by distance learning while I was very young, and went on to complete a bachelor's degree the same way. I never had any doubt that education was important and was something that should be taken seriously.

But things weren't always rosy. My parents divorced when I was 11. And while this was initially a source of curiosity for me (I loved even then that something 'exciting' was going on in my family), it was really hard on my Mum. At that time, women weren't usually involved in financial matters, and tended not to be named on mortgages, or utility bills, or finance agreements. So there was a long period of time when Mum was trying to figure it all out, and make it all work, with three young girls to support and no real income.

Mum was always very open with me about what was going on, and I guess there's a sense to which I stepped into a 'parental-support' role. I knew how much things cost, and how little we had. I knew how hard it was for Mum, and became very mindful of what we couldn't afford to do – to the extent that I often made these decisions for myself, without even raising it with Mum, because I didn't want her to be worried… and I knew what the answer would be.

I remember quite distinctly, while I was at high school, I entered the local performing arts competitions, playing piano, but we couldn't afford to photocopy the sheet music – so I had one copy – my copy. But of course the judges need a copy. That was OK, I could play the piece from memory – so I gave them mine…

I think you can probably imagine what happened. Complete mental block part way through the piece. No sheet music to keep me grounded or find my place. It was mortifying.

I grew up fast, and took on responsibility for things from an early age. And from this emerged a very deep-rooted sense of self-reliance. To this day I feel uncomfortable if I am dependent on somebody else for anything.

My parents (both when they were together and after they separated) were inconsistent disciplinarians. Some days a particular behaviour was funny – and we'd all have a laugh. The next day it warranted a severe telling off. Or worse. And what bothered me most about this was how unfair it was. Fairness became a very important value for me, stemming I believe from these childhood experiences. Consistency and fairness really matter to me, and I don't like witnessing or being party to things that are inconsistent or unfair. But it also means that I can have quite an emotional response if I believe I'm being treated unfairly.

I was a pretty clever kid. Luckily for me, with a mother who cared so much about the value of education, she pushed me. And she pushed my schools and teachers. There was always an extension class, or an additional subject or something that was extending me academically. She also prevented me from leaving school in sixth form to join the Airforce (thanks Mum!) and she encouraged me to move away from the small town I grew up in to go to University.

Interestingly, though, my cleverness was in pattern recognition, mostly. I was good at maths, and music, and science. I could find the patterns and predict the outcome. I never saw myself as particularly creative, and I wasn't that interested in doing something highly specialised. I didn't like to close down options. It annoyed me when I had to narrow down my school subject selection to just a handful of electives. I wanted to do all of them. In the end, I chose to do some subjects a year early so that I could take extra subjects the following year. I remember one teacher suggested I should retake School Certificate maths, and get an even better mark. I had already received an A – I couldn't even begin to fathom what could be gained from getting a higher mark, when the result would still be recorded as an A!

I specifically remember while I was at intermediate school, thanks to my Mum's encouragement, the school principal got me enrolled in a maths extension class operated out of Otago University. Each week, I'd receive five maths problems to solve, and I had to mail them back to be graded.

The funny thing was, I was doing it entirely independently. Usually at home in the evenings. And I always got the answers right. But I could never show my workings. I didn't have any grasp of calculus, or algebra, or complex geometry. I was 12. I hadn't taken any other extension classes, or read any additional theory. Somehow I was able to find the pattern and arrive at the answer, but I lacked the mathematical language to explain how I arrived there.

Needless to say, I found receiving a mark of 5/25 for getting the answers right but not showing my workings, incredibly unfair!

This pattern started cropping up in my working life too, though, so at some point I had to take notice…

I cared about solving big problems, and I could work out viable solutions. The only problem was, nobody else could see how I got there, so they didn't know whether the answer was going to work.

My brain is quick, and I solve problems by looking at the underlying patterns and systems at play. Luckily, I learned in my early thirties that the real effort wasn't in solving the problem itself, but in implementing the solution, and that this required me to take the time to figure out how I got there. Or more importantly, how other people could get there. To reverse engineer my process, and make it simple and accessible.

I think my desire to have massive impact stems from my recognition that I couldn't fix my own family, but perhaps I could fix things so that other people's families might not be broken. That I couldn't stop my dad from being violent, but perhaps I could teach young men skills that would prevent them from resorting to violence. That I couldn't help my mum find a well-paying job, but maybe I could figure out why some people find it really hard – even when they're qualified and well-intentioned – to fit the mould of corporate working life, and consequently are consigned to poorer-paying jobs that don't make full use of their skills.

So drawing from these memories, I arrived at my 'why'. I want to fix the world. All of it.

Am I Pollyanna-ish? You bet. Am I an idealist? I wouldn't have it any other way. My greatest fear in the whole world? Not having the impact I know I'm capable of.

But the audacious thing is, I actually believe I can, and I will. Not all at once, and (in spite of my tendency to try and do it alone) with help from others…

Which is where you come in.

I found my 'why', at age 38. And it changed me. It made my entire life to this point make sense. It made *me* make sense.

I'm determined that you should have the same opportunity…

2. Finding Your Inspiration

*"Character cannot be developed in ease and quiet.
Only through experience of trial and suffering can the
soul be strengthened, ambition inspired, and success
achieved." Helen Keller*

Inspiration can be illusive. Something that you see from the corner of your eye, but by the time you've turned to look for it, it's gone… it's moved on to somewhere else or someone else.

For many people, inspiration becomes something that used to exist, perhaps when they were a child, or a teenager. Some people are lucky enough that it persisted into their college years or the first few years in their career. But for many, inspiration left them long ago. It's been relegated to the shelf, along with creativity, as something that 'other people' have.

That's really sad.

So in this section we're going to talk about why you should be inspired, where you might find sources of inspiration, and ultimately, we're going to work through two key tools that I use with my clients to tap into their inspiration.

But before we do that, let's get a little bit clearer about inspiration. Specifically, I want to help you see that inspiration isn't something that's for 'other people', but actually is something that you can foster and cultivate.

Why Should You Be Inspired?

My answer to this is simple. Because the *world* needs you to be inspired.

There are lots of broken things around us. Broken people, broken systems, broken promises, broken companies.

These broken things won't be fixed just by leaving them alone. They also won't be fixed just by complaining about them, unless that complaint is incredibly constructive and directed to somebody who has the means and the inspiration to do something about it.

Also, *you* need you to be inspired. You have one life. Just one. And it is comparatively short. You deserve to lead that life with inspiration fuelling you. It was never intended that people would enter the world to lead soul-less, uninspired and joy-destroying lives.

And the good news is that by understanding what inspiration is, you can start to see the simple steps involved in turning your everyday experiences into a source of inspiration and an impetus to do something about it.

Observation

The first thing that needs to happen is that you need to 'see' that there is a problem. Whether it's a rocky relationship with a co-worker, an unwanted development in your town or neighbourhood, or a national crisis, you can't do anything about it if you don't know it exists.

So the starting point to finding inspiration is actually looking for it.

Mindfulness

How many times have you realised you've been walking past something every day and never actually *seen* it. You're too busy thinking about the meeting that you have to attend when you get to work, or the fight you had with your partner before you left the house, or what you're going to have for dinner tonight.

Most of us spend most of our lives stuck in our own heads, and not actually living in the world. So to find our inspiration, we not only have to be looking for it, but we have to foster the mindfulness to actually *see* it when it's there.

Reflection

So we're progressing along our journey towards inspiration, and we know we want to find some, and we know we have to be alert and mindful if we are to spot it, which is a great start. But then you actually have to do something with it, mentally, once it's in your head.

You have to process it. Ponder it. Chew it around. You have to reflect on it with purpose.

Dissatisfaction

So after all of that, what is a useful working definition of inspiration that gets us away from a fluffy ethereal thing that may or may not show up – like a muse – when we least expect it? For me, the answer is **dissatisfaction**. As unexciting as that sounds.

- Dissatisfaction is a **gap** between where something is, and where something *should* be.

- Dissatisfaction is a **divide** between how something works, and how it *could* work.
- Dissatisfaction is a **frustration** with how something unfolds, and how it *could* have unfolded.
- Dissatisfaction is a **sense of emptiness** between what exists, and what you know *could* exist.

These are your sources of inspiration. The fuel for your muse.

It could come from people, feelings, places, events, and objects. It can come from memories, desires, pain, creativity, or simply wanting tomorrow to be better than today.

Regardless of the source, there's a degree of dissatisfaction required.

So now you might be thinking that sounds pretty negative. Who wants to live their life wandering around looking for things to be unhappy about?

The answer is no-one. Well actually some people do appear to want this, but I'm sure if you asked them, they'd say they didn't.

The good news is these sources can be positive as well as negative. How you frame them is up to you. Have you ever heard it said that where the pessimist sees problems, the optimist seems opportunities? It's a bit like that. I actually don't mind whether you use negativity or positivity to fuel your inspiration *provided* your pessimism doesn't stand in the way of you turning your inspiration into a decision to act. In other words, it doesn't work for you if you go from "gosh – there's a problem over there" to "… but it can't be fixed" without deeply engaging in the fact that it **can** be improved.

And in fact, having seen the problem, you have an obligation to try and help.

In fact, it's actually hard to sustain inspiration when it's framed in a negative way, so even if the problem is really bad, and the status quo is terrible, focusing on what could be better rather than what is currently wrong will typically be more likely to keep you going through the tough bits.

Spotlight: Powerful Questions

"Successful people ask better questions, and as a result, they get better answers" Tony Robbins

Before we get too much deeper into what your inspiration might be, I want to introduce you to my favourite punctuation mark: the question mark. This is vital because so much of your personal power lies in asking yourself the right questions – at the right times. So bear with me while we take a minor detour – it will serve you well.

It is entirely possible that the most powerful thing in the world is the humble question mark. Whether written, or spoken, it has the potential to create revolutionary change, turn mice into men and bring dictators to their knees.

How?

By creating a gap. (Do you see what I did there!)

A powerful, searching, probing gap. And gaps are important, because they create space. Space to reflect. Space to reexamine. Space to ponder. Space to acknowledge. Space to listen.

But they need to be *open* questions. Questions that open up the mind rather than closing it down. Not questions that can be answered with a simple yes or no. And not questions that can readily be answered with a factual response.

The Internal Question

Our minds are rich with monologue but we don't always notice it. We explain events around us, to ourselves. We legitimise actions we're about to take, to ourselves. We play out what might happen next, to ourselves.

And when bad things happen to us, we verbalise our thoughts, feelings and reactions, inside our heads.

Sometimes this is in the form of statements: "gosh, I didn't expect that", or "I know what not to do next time". Sometimes, though, it takes the form of questions: "why did this happen to me?" or "how did I end up here?". Questions like this make you the victim. They reinforce the idea that something was done to you.

But the very best questions? They require you to start problem-solving. They spur you to action. They create a *gap* between your present gloomy mood and a new space where you can begin to turn your thinking, and your situation, around:

- "What can I learn from this?"
- "What can I do to come back stronger as a result of this temporary set-back?"
- "What steps, if I took them right now, would prevent this from happening again?"

Recognising your internal monologue is not always easy. Especially if it is a persistent chatter, always in your mind. Chances are you have consciously stopped listening to it... but it's still there, and your subconscious brain still pays attention. So you need to practice mindfulness, and get better at recognising when your internal monologue is taking you in an unhelpful direction, and *deliberately* turn things around through the power of a high quality internal question.

The Rhetorical Question

A rhetorical question is a literary device used to emphasise or illustrate a point. Simply put, it is a question to which no answer is actually expected.

In order to be effective, a rhetorical question has to be followed by a brief pause – a **gap** – where the speaker allows the audience (or the writer allows the reader) to contemplate the answer and appreciate the purpose of the question.

What is the realisation that it creates? What is the 'a-ha' moment? Does it demonstrate a hypocrisy you hold? Or a flawed belief?

It is the **gap** that is important here. It is that gap that requires you to try and answer the question – and then consider what the question and answer mean in context.

The Coaching Question

If you manage staff, or coach others, or rely on others to get things done, the power of questions cannot be overstated.

It is easy when you are in a position of authority to think that this means you need to have all the answers. But actually, the opposite is true. If you have great questions, you don't need any of the answers.

BUT this is really hard. Your brain loves to answer questions. It can't help itself! When your team member asks you a question, your brain immediately leaps to find an answer... to demonstrate your expertise, to justify your position in the relationship and just to make you feel more confident. But answering these questions is not helping.

You need to rewire your brain, and learn to respond with a question of your own. Try:

- "What do you think?"
- "How do you feel about that?"
- "What do you think the options are?"
- "What is your intuition telling you?"
- "What would you need to do to find out?"

These questions result in two new gaps. The gap you need to create between the question you've been asked and how you respond, and a gap in the mind of the person asking the first question and thinking about answering your question.

Your employee will gain far more from answering the question themselves than they ever will from being given the answer – even if your answer was brilliant!

The Strategic Question

Both an internal and an external question – but one of the most important question categories... "Why?"

"Why are you in business?"

"Why were you put on this earth?"

There are, of course, subsets of these questions, but until you've answered your own 'why' the lesser questions will merely be distractions.

Once you've created this gap and answered your 'why' you can figure out:

- Where do you need to be in five, 10, 20 years?
- What do you need to do to get there?
- How are you going to do it?

And the answers to these questions are very important, but without identifying your 'why', the answers will probably be wrong.

By the way, the funniest thing about 'why' questions is that they don't work. You actually have to find a way to ask them as a 'what' question. 'Why' sets your brain up for an argument... "why did you do that?", "why are you home late?" And so forth. Instead you need to pause for a minute, and reframe the question as a 'what'. Clearly not all 'why' questions are intended to provoke a defensive response, but your brain doesn't care, and gets prepared regardless. Try "what led you to do that?" or "what would you need to do differently to be home on time in the future?" Subtle, but important.

Questioning Assumptions

Possibly the most important thing you can understand about your own brain? It *loves* shortcuts. If it can find a way to streamline your thinking process, it will. It constantly creates categories and rules to help you understand the world around you. Some of these rules and categories are incredibly helpful. Like, "food that is mouldy is probably not good to eat".

And yet we eat blue cheese, which is mouldy – in a good way. So we build these mental schemas and rules that *mostly* help us make sense of the world around us.

But sometimes, these assumptions are *unconscious* and *untested*. We simply aren't even aware we are making an assumption, let alone whether or not it is accurate. So one of my favourite questions of all gets right to the heart of these untested unconscious assumptions.

"In order for this to happen like I expect, what must be true?"

You might discover you are assuming another person will do something, so you don't need to, but your success depends on it being done.

You might discover you are assuming that the current technology trends will continue.

You might discover you are assuming people wearing dirty ripped jeans can't afford high-end designer clothing.

I guarantee that if you create the **gap** between what you think you're about to do, ask yourself this question, and then course-correct, you'll find opportunities and possibilities that you didn't imagine possible, because your own mind was closing them off to you.

We're now going to complete two exercises that can help you find your own inspiration.

Write A Ten Year Vision

Don't worry if you don't see yourself as a writer, perfect prose is not the purpose of this exercise!

I want you to find 30 minutes to an hour of time in your schedule where you can be genuinely uninterrupted. No children, no social media, no phone calls. Take out a blank notebook, or open a new document on your computer and get ready to… just… write. Stream of consciousness. No editing, no re-reading. No stopping to think. No planning.

I want you to close your eyes for a minute before you start and imagine that you are waking up in the morning, 10 years in the future. Maybe write down the date, just as a centering thought, so you know where you are in time. Now daydream about your life as it would be if: you had absolutely no fear, nothing could go wrong, and money was no object. I'm deeply serious.

Think about where you'd be (in the world, in your house) and who you'd be with. Think about what you would be doing if you absolutely knew that nothing could go wrong. Remember this is your perfect life. Not anyone else's. Perhaps start by waking up – what do you see around you when you wake? Is it early, or is it late? Who is with you? What are they doing? What does your room look like? Are you even in a room? Is the room in a house? Or an apartment? Or a hotel? What do you do when you get up? Do you have a comfortable ideal routine that you slip into? Do you exercise? Do you eat breakfast? What do you have?

Keep examining this future life and write it all down as you go.

What do you do during the day? Who do you spend time with? What work are you doing? What play? Do you have pets? How do you feel? About your family? About your life? About money? About your professional direction? Are you being impactful? Are you somebody important? To whom? How much money do you have? Does it come easily to you? How do you behave? Are you generous? Are you hard-working? Are you relaxed? Are you busy? Are you fit? Are you healthy? What do you enjoy eating?

When I did this, I had a chauffeur, a chef and a housekeeper – which is a long way from my present reality – so don't worry if it seems ludicrous or unlikely – just keep going.

Keep going through the whole day. Although it works well as a 'diary' don't forget to include the tangential details that make it real – like the why, and the what happens next. Are you in your office writing today, because next week you're heading overseas to speak at a conference? Are you entertaining clients who will ultimately create prosperity for your business? There are no limitations except your own imagination. The only 'grounding' advice is, this needs to be a description of something you really would like to have. That if it were possible (and don't worry about whether it's possible or not), you could look at it and say – 'that's perfect'.

Details are really important here, it doesn't need to be perfectly written, but it needs to have evocative details. I love the smell of lilies, so for me, my future house always has fresh lilies in the hallway. Do you want to travel? Well you might not fit all the travel you want into the one day you choose to write about, but you can certainly be reviewing plans for a major trip. You could be reviewing your itinerary for the next 12 months. Do you love having extended family close by? They may not all visit your lovely home on the day in question, but you could speak to them on the phone and discuss travel arrangements.

Keep going until you fall into bed, tired but happy, in the evening of this perfect day. Reflect back on how it made you feel.

Now at this point, you can edit – but not to remove details, only to improve readability and flow. Clunky grammar that throws you out of the moment while you read? That has to go. The extravagant caviar canapés with champagne that you ate at the gallery opening you hosted? That stays.

Remember – this exercise is all about your most outrageous wishes and desires. Just a quick note though – it doesn't have to be extravagant. I've used examples like that to prove a point here, but actually, it's just as important that, given this is *your* dream, you include solitude, and simplicity, and calm, if that is what you seek.

Now you are welcome to polish a little bit, but the core ethos of what you wrote needs to remain. If I popped over and you showed me the first draft, and your final product, they need to be related to each other!

So what's the point of all this, I hear you ask.

As children, even children with some pretty difficult circumstances, we have few inhibitions on what we think is possible when we grow up. Children can dream of being princesses, or fire-fighters or Princess-Fire-fighters. They don't filter their expectations based on what society thinks is likely for them, because of their family background, or upbringing, or financial circumstances. But as we get older, these inhibitions – that 'society' and our families create for us – start to become an inbuilt feature of who we think we are. They become part of our monologue. We take over ownership for them, and start to assume they are real. That they are 'true'.

For me, this was the case. My Mum definitely expected me to be successful, but that was within the bounds of her experiences. That meant going to University (something that was relatively unheard of in my family) and getting a high paying job. But that was about it. And the scale of what constituted high paying was a bit underdone. A six-figure salary was about the pinnacle of what my family could imagine. And let's be clear, that came with some baggage too!

"People with money aren't happy." "People with money aren't very nice." "Money is always a struggle." "Having a job is important." "Without a job, life is tough."

Now all of these things *can* be true. But they aren't immutable facts. They don't have to be true. And they definitely don't have to be true for me. The purpose of this exercise is to try and get underneath these constraints that are placed on us – by ourselves, and by those around us. And the very act of writing it down, starts to make it tangible. Starts to make it real… Starts to make it less scary and distant.

I learned about this technique listening to Tim Ferriss interview Debbie Millman on a podcast. Millman is a highly successful designer. Her career has brought her significant acclaim, with Fast Company naming her "one of the most creative people in business", and Graphic Design USA calling her "one of the most influential designers working today". She is also an author, educator, curator and hosts the podcast *Design Matters*. This exercise was something that she was given as an assignment for a design class she was taking. It no doubt seemed a rather odd assignment at the time.

With the benefit of hindsight, and numerous other case studies (Debbie remained close to the professor, and knows this for a fact), extraordinarily large chunks of these assignments would come true for their authors. Not through magic, but through the clarity of goals and purpose that writing them down creates.

Please take the time to complete this exercise now. When you're finished, print it out, and keep it somewhere you can refer to it frequently.

So now you have a relatively holistic vision for the future. On a personal level at least, you are more clear about what your values and preferences are as it pertains to life around you – your friends, family and circumstances. But there will also be some clues in this story about your future self that shed *some* light on the hopes you have for the world outside your immediate surrounds. Don't worry too much if these aren't clear. In fact don't worry if there appear to be none at all. Sometimes these vision statements make more sense as the reality starts to unfold.

Now it is time to get out our second tool...

Find Your 'Why'

In 2009, Simon Sinek wrote a book called *Start With Why*. At its core, it is a book about how the human brain works. It is a book about why the logical brain, which we all like to think is in charge of our day-to-day decision-making, is actually not in charge at all.

Sinek's premise, which is backed by psychological evidence, is that our emotional brains are actually calling the shots, but are quite happy for us not to be aware of this fact, and allow us to fool ourselves that there's a logical explanation for why you bought that new big screen television, even though you couldn't really afford it.

Drawing on anecdotes and evidence from the corporate sector, Sinek outlines how people "don't buy *what* you do, they buy ***why you do it.***" And this path of being clear and communicating your 'why' to others, is the path by which you can create brand loyalty and customer engagement on a massive level.

Why do so many people buy Apple products when they aren't *always* the best, and their company philosophy sometimes means that the bugs haven't been fully ironed out before they go to market… and they're definitely not the most affordable?

Because people don't buy *what* Apple does, they buy *why they do it*.

Funnily enough, the converse is also true. There are a large number of people who don't buy Apple products. And often, these 'non-believers' are incredibly ardent in their rejection of the brand. They will go onto a post about the pending release of a new Apple product and vociferously decry the overpriced, over-engineered, over-designed, over-secretive... you get the picture. They will probably promote an alternative, but actually the bulk of their verbiage is spent on 'anti-Apple' not pro-something-else. If you asked them, many of these folks would say it's because they haven't bought into the hype and they use rationality and logic to decide what's the best product for them.

I'm sceptical. Reason, rationality and logic doesn't lead you to hate a product. It definitely doesn't compel you to write a 1,000 word essay about everything that's wrong with that product, and it doesn't lead you to hurl names and abuse at those who *do* buy the product on the basis that they're unthinking lemmings being brainwashed into the corporate marketing machine that is Apple.

I would suggest that anti-Apple sentiment (or any other brand-rejection that becomes emotionally driven) is coming from the exact same place... And is likely driven by a desire to be contrary. A certain desire to defy the perceived majority and do the opposite. Anti-conformity, anti-establishment, and anti-hype. And I have no problem with that. People are entitled to be passionate about whatever they like (within reason). I just would like it if they didn't pretend it stemmed from some higher-level thinking or superior intellect! Because in reality, it's coming from exactly the same place.

Now one of the greatest frustrations about Sinek's book is that it sets up this phenomenal case for the power of our emotional brains to take over our decision-making *if* we can connect to them with language and/or symbolism, but never helps you figure out what your 'why' actually is. Irrespective of whether it's you the person, you the founder of your own company/venture or a multinational conglomerate. You finish the book with a certain sense of 'now what?'

Fortunately, between *Start With Why* and Sinek's wildly popular TEDx talk, two individuals compelled by their *own* 'why', managed to reach out to him (I don't actually know this, it might have been the other way round, but it sounds like a good story!) to say, 'we've got some ideas about *how* to find your 'why'...'

...And *Find Your Why* was published in 2017.

It outlines a range of workshop methods for finding your 'why'. Whether you want to find your personal 'why' or that of your team, or ultimately, that of the company you work for, there's a methodology for achieving that.

On a quiet afternoon in October 2017, a few days after my copy of the book arrived, I found my 'why'. And the rest, as they say, is history.

Funnily enough, I was too impatient to read the whole book, and I kind of worked my way towards it. The most important thing, though, is to work with a 'companion'. You are too close to your own life to see the patterns and themes. And those patterns and themes are exactly what you need to see and unpick to figure out what the symbols and emotions are that are driving you. What makes you tick is something that you'll intuitively grasp when you see it written down, but it isn't something that you can just 'think about for a few hours' and magically find.

Actually, that's not quite true. Probably some people can do that. Perhaps even Sinek himself, given that he hadn't met David Mead and Peter Docker (the co-authors of *Find Your Why*) at the time that he found his own 'why'…

The process matters. So do buy the book. You won't regret it.

At its core, though, you spend some time drawing out and describing a handful of memories that you believe defined you. Events that made you the person you are today. There's a reason these memories stand out with greater clarity and significance for you than others. There's a reason why the time you got lost at the shopping mall, but found a policeman who helped you find your Mum stands out more than what you had for dinner on the night before you started school.

The reason is relatively simple – it's because of the depth and power of the emotions that are attached to them.

Cognitive psychology spends a great deal of time grappling with human memory. How it works, how memories are formed. Where they are stored. And how they are recalled. There are many practical applications for this knowledge. Helping people deal with trauma. Understanding whether or not eye-witness testimony should be relied upon in the criminal justice system, understanding and finding treatments for diseases like Alzheimer's, and helping people to learn new information for their jobs or study.

We know from this excellent and expanding body of work that memories are very fragile. They can be edited, changed, and can even be lost completely. But we also know that most memories, once formed, aren't completely lost; we simply lose the ability to recall them. Recall, it turns out, is what matters most when it comes to memory.

Novelty helps. The more unusual and uncommon the event, the more likely it is that a memory will be formed, because your emotional brain is working hard to figure out if this previously unencountered situation poses you any danger. Novelty also means that the handful of 'triggers' that are attached to the memory once it is formed, are also likely to have more salience, and stand out more. For example, if you went to Disneyland once as a child, everything about that trip will be attached to one memory. The feeling of hugging a giant Mickey Mouse. The thrill of Space Mountain. The smell of the hotel room you stayed in. The colour of the fireworks. The sounds of the parade... Chances are high that if you heard another person try and describe one of these characteristics, a lot of this memory would come flooding back to you. The more senses are involved (sights, sounds, smells, tastes and touch) the more likely you are to recall it. The more emotion that is attached, the more likely you are to recall it.

(Incidentally, this knowledge can be used in reverse... for more on how to *create* defining memories, check out *The Power of Moments* by Chip Heath and Dan Heath.)

Also, though, the more often you call the memory to mind – to recount it to your friends at school, to describe it to your grandma who couldn't come, to remember it fondly with mum and dad, or even to argue about who got the longest hug from Mickey with your older sibling – the easier this memory will be to recall. But there is a risk with this. Each time you bring this memory 'out' to look at it, feel it, talk about it, you can also inadvertently (or even intentionally) change it. If your big sister conveys frequently enough, and emphatically enough, with sufficient detail, the extent to which her hug was longer than yours, eventually seeds of doubt will be sown, and potentially, over time, your family (and even you) start to believe that it is true.

There is an entire sub-discipline within psychology that is focused on memory, and its creation, re-creation and fallibility. Prominent psychologist and researcher, Elizabeth Loftus, of the University of California, Irvine, has demonstrated over numerous experiments in the lab, and also in the field, how malleable and subject to manipulation our memories are. Especially if there is photographic 'evidence', which in the era of Photoshop and digital photography is not particularly difficult to engineer. This characteristic malleability is both useful, and frightening. Useful in terms of understanding our own brains and how they work, but frightening when you consider how persuasive eyewitness testimony is in the context of our justice system. The way a police officer questions a witness immediately after an event can deeply alter the 'memory' the eyewitness has for the event. We are subject to suggestion, and we all have a built-in desire to please. When properly undertaken, the capturing of eyewitness testimony can be useful, but even in the act of creating a line-up for an eye-witness to view, there can be unintended consequences. History is littered with falsely accused people being incorrectly identified as the perpetrator from a poorly conducted line-up.

So why does such an unreliable medium as memory serve as the gateway in to understanding and figuring out our 'why'?

Largely it's because the memory itself doesn't matter. It could be anything really. A vivid recollection of a purple lollypop or a deeply traumatic car accident. What actually matters is the emotional significance you have attached to it. Irrespective of whether it's true, partially true, or entirely false, you *believe* it's true, and you have a suite of associated emotions and feelings attached to it. It has become part of your narrative. You have made it a part of who you are.

But you may not understand why.

The area of our brain responsible for forming memories, the hippocampus, is part of a larger brain region known as the limbic system. The limbic system is responsible for, among other things, our emotional state and regulation. It is not responsible for language or logic. While it is true that it can be involved in these activities, it cannot create the act of verbalising... your frontal cortex *accesses* this system when it tries to put emotions into words.

You know the saying "lost for words"? In large part, this 'disconnect' between the emotional centres of our brain, and the areas responsible for logic, and sense-making, and decision-making, and language, is what this saying is referring to. You can be entirely overwhelmed – positively or negatively – by an experience, yet struggle to put it into words.

So let's talk about communication for a minute – we're going to go into more detail in a later chapter, because communication is vital for impact – but in the meantime, I just would like you to think about the miracle that is our ability to communicate with other people through the formation of language.

Let's say you have an inspired idea, and you want to get others excited about it. Neurons are firing left, right and centre (literally) and you're excited, emotional, and eager to show someone else the absolute awesomeness of your idea.

While you are thinking about what to say, messages are firing back and forth between your emotional brain and your logical brain. You're probably not aware of it, because it happens so quick, but you're rehearsing a handful of options for what to say to find the one that you believe will properly convey the awesomeness of the concept. You discard a handful of ideas as 'too naff' or dull, and ultimately you arrive at a serious contender. Before you even open your mouth to speak, you have been observing/participating in a brain that is 'playing tennis' back and forth between these two parts of your brain. It's an incredibly rich and dynamic emotional world. Everything is awesome.

Now think about language for a minute. It's magnificent when well-wielded, but can be absolutely butchered as well. There is nothing intrinsic to language that is emotional, or in some cases even meaningful. The word 'happy' doesn't really describe what happiness is. Even the word 'ecstatic' doesn't do the *experience* of ecstasy, justice.

What is actually happening that makes these words meaningful is entirely internal to our own brain. That tennis match I mentioned – that's where a word 'evokes' something for you. And what it evokes for you won't be the same as what it evokes for me. In a room of 100 people I would put money on 100 different 'experiences' of these words.

So when you really boil it down, communication – even just between two individuals, which is possibly the most basic type – takes a rich, dynamic suite of concepts and emotions and 'boils them down' to a two-dimensional essence in the form of some words (and some body language) to be conveyed to somebody else. That person then takes this low-fi rendition of your amazing idea, and tries to reconstitute it using their own memories and experiences – which, in most cases, are completely different from yours.

What could possibly go wrong!

To be quite honest, language is one area of human endeavour that has not really evolved at all over the last 100,000 years or so. Even with the introduction of computers, AI and robotics, we aren't any closer to figuring out how we human beings can share the full richness of our emotional inner worlds with each other. That may be a good thing...[*]

Now all of this might seem a little bit gloomy. But that's where the sheer brilliance of the *Find Your Why* method comes to the fore. It recognises that the memories themselves aren't what actually

---

[*] If this interests you, please check out "Wait, but Why?" and Elon Musk's work on the Brain Machine Interface at https://waitbutwhy.com/2017/04/neuralink.html. It will blow your mind – plus it has stick-figures!

matters, but the *significance* you attach to them holds clues to your 'why'. It also recognises the inherent difficulties we have in verbalising our emotional world – I mean, let's face it, unless you're a brilliant narrator or novelist, your communication is likely to be less evocative and three-dimensional than you want it to be – and it creates a framework, to overcome this. Using a companion, and providing that companion with a range of questions and prompts they can use to help you narrow in on the emotional core of these memories, so that, together, you might get closer to identifying how these memories hold the key to what makes **you** tick.

Following the process, you identify themes, which you can then explore in a bit more detail – and you iterate the language as you go. For example, one of the themes I came up with initially was problem-solving. It's a big part of who I am, and the problems need to be the *actual* causes, not just the symptoms of the problems. But as we worked through the process, I started to feel that problem-solving didn't really capture it, but impact came a lot closer. So you can play with the words – you're looking for something that makes you feel as close as possible to that inner world you tried to describe to your companion. Something that resonates for you.

Ultimately, you start turning these themes and concepts into your 'why' statement: To _____ (contribution), so that _____ (impact).

My why?

To help people lead inspired, intentional, impactful lives, so that, together, we can resolve the broken pieces.

Intuitively I'd always been searching for these words – grasping at threads of them, but never quite reaching it. And to be fair, I'm still 'living' with these words. They may alter again as that process unfolds, but for now, I'm pretty happy. I'm inspired.

Heck, I'm inspired enough to write a book about it!

So now you have completed two different exercises – writing your 10-year vision and *Finding Your Why*. By now you should be feeling pretty inspired! But you may be wondering why I've introduced you to two tools…

And that's a great question – in fact either one of them on their own is pretty powerful! But there is a reason. I want you to go back to your vision now, and re-read it now that you've found your 'why'. You need to ensure that you can reconcile the two, because there will be differences between them – at least at first blush. You may find that you want to re-word or add slightly to your vision statement in light of knowing your 'why'. That's fine.

You may also come across a word in your vision statement that is more potent for you than something in your 'why' statement, so you change that as well. That's also fine.

But what you're really looking for are the threads that connect them. In a sense, you're looking to validate your vision for the future against your 'why'.

I worked with a client whose 'why' statement was a deeply poignant and evocative statement about connecting people with their happiest memories – about capturing them for posterity and ensuring they could recall them when times got tough. Yet his vision was to be successful in a leadership role at the firm he already worked for. At first glance, these two things seem somewhat at odds with each other. In fact he had come to me for help specifically because he was struggling to understand leadership, as separate from his technical and specialist knowledge in his line of work – an incredibly common malady for experts who are promoted into leadership.

But as we worked through the reconciling process, it became really clear that the organisation he worked for **had the same 'why'**. And consequently, being successful as a senior leader in that organisation meant that he was influencing decision-making and strategy in a way that multiplied his impact – he was better able to achieve his own 'why' by aligning with the resources and impact of an organisation that was already doing it. As soon as this connection was apparent, the journey to effective leadership became a lot simpler. He was able to start to see the tasks that leaders perform – leading strategy development, communicating vision to team members, supporting his leadership team colleagues – as directly influencing his 'why', their importance and significance became clearer, and his motivation to learn these skills, rather than relying solely on his technical expertise, became strong, and he was prepared to put in the effort to learn them. Prior to this 'aha' moment, these leadership skills had been a distraction from his purpose. And as you can probably imagine, a deep source of frustration, because they didn't come naturally for him.

Sources Of Inspiration Juice

Just to round out the topic of inspiration, I want to touch on some tangential sources of inspiration. This is important, because your 'why' and your vision will get you so far, but from time to time, particularly when you are emotionally or physically depleted, you will need to recharge, and reconnect. So below I've collected a number of places (both metaphorical and physical) where you might find some extra oomph when you need it.

People

Fortunately not in short supply, the world is full of people. So look to them for sources of inspiration. Remember that people can provide both positive and negative inspiration: examples of what to do, and also examples of what **not** to do; examples of how to overcome adversity, and how not to; examples of good leadership, and terrible leadership; examples of living with purpose and purposelessness.

I know, for example, that I've learned far more about leadership from my terrible bosses than I have from my fabulous bosses – besides which, terrible bosses are – unfortunately – much more common! But there are things that a bad boss can't teach you, because you don't notice them in their absence. A bad boss might be atrocious at displaying gratitude when you do a good job, but this might be simply that he never thanks you for your work. But without the great boss's example, you'll never know the power of a simple thank you message at the end of a hectic day.

Places

There are places on earth that are majestic and breathtaking, and there are places on earth that are sobering and depressing. Both these extremes probably exist, in some way, right in your hometown. And both can be deeply compelling sources of inspiration.

Getting out in nature can be incredibly beneficial for recharging, as can wondering through a poor part of town and reflecting upon what you might do to help, or being grateful for what you have, or determined that this calamity won't befall your family.

Getting away from your normal environment can also be deeply inspiring, just seeing places you haven't seen before can trigger a whole fresh burst of ideas and creativity that may have been lacking.

You don't necessarily need to go all the way to the Grand Canyon or the Pyramids at Giza to be blown away by the diverse richness of our world, and to recharge your inspiration.

Events

I really like this one because it can be as elaborate or as simple as you make it. From participating in events in your local community, to creating an event for others to participate in, to reading about events that happened in the past, and reflecting on the circumstances, people and happenstance that led to that event being sufficiently momentous that someone wrote about it.

For example, I recently re-read (because it was something we learnt in school) Kate Sheppard's story, the woman who led the campaign (and the petition) to gain New Zealand women the right to vote in the General Election. Upon re-reading, the thing that struck me most was the sheer monumental task of obtaining 32,000 signatures on a petition at a time when there were only a handful of telephones, no internet, no motor vehicles and no aeroplane travel. So by horse and carriage, telegram and ship, this phenomenal woman built a team, and travelled the length and breadth of New Zealand persuading people to sign a petition, to do something that, until that point, was completely unheard of in the entire world.

Luckily for us, the history books are littered with stories of remarkable achievement – and diabolical tyranny – both of which can inspire you in their own way.

Problems

Now I'm not really one for dwelling on negative things, and problems can sound like negative things, but with the right mindset, problems become opportunities and sources of inspiration pretty quickly, especially if you ask the right questions.

Problems can be 'mini', like being frustrated that you can't find a particular product or service in your local area: and let's face it, you'll probably cope if this problem doesn't get solved... Through to 'maxi', like child poverty, or famine, or climate change.

But the purpose of examining these problems isn't to get depressed and sad. It's to ask questions about what you could do to fix it. Literally, "what could I do to solve this problem, in part or whole"?

Questions are powerful – hence why I included the "spotlight" section on questions earlier. They are the keys to unlocking what your brain is capable of. Now I hear you sounding sceptical. Let me explain a little of the psychology behind your brain's response to questions.

Have you ever noticed that when someone comes to you with a question – or even when someone presents you with a problem they're facing, and you sense they want some help – your brain automatically and unconsciously starts answering the question or solving the problem. It's been the subject of many jokes about relationships – that women raise issues or problems with their significant other (it's the jokes that generalise, not me) and the man starts answering the question or solving the problem, when actually all that was wanted was a sympathetic ear!

Your brain's default position is to answer questions. It's part of our conversation – if someone says 'how are you?" you don't ignore it, you answer, even when you don't particularly know the person.

Questions *compel* answers. So ask good questions. Because the better the questions you ask – out loud or inside your head – the better the answers your brain will provide.

If you ask "why do things like this always happen to me?" you brain will provide you with dozens of answers as to why these things happen to you... because you lack this or that, because you're not dynamic enough, because you aren't respected, because... because... because. But if, instead, the question you asked was "what can I learn from this?" you get different answers to the exact same situation. If you ask "how can I use this experience to drive me forward and achieve my goals?" you get yet different answers.

Practicing mindfulness will help you to spot these opportunities, because your brain has had a life-time of practice with the 'default' questions – so deliberately changing your questions to be more empowering can take a bit of practice!

Design Thinking

In addition to asking great questions, there are proven techniques used to create innovative and creative approaches to problem-solving. Edward de Bono specialises in creating breakthrough creative problem-solving and lateral thinking techniques, Jeanne Liedtka promotes the use of design as a metaphor for problem-solving of all kinds, and there are many more besides.

Try 'merging' two apparently unrelated disciplines and see what happens. I studied strategic studies for my Master's degree, which was a slightly odd mix of security policy (transnational crime, terrorism studies, foreign policy et cetera) and futures thinking. It was the futures thinking papers that got me the most enthusiastic, although some of the other topics were incredibly interesting. I wrote my Master's thesis on the ways that architecture is like futures thinking. Initially it was just a crazy idea, but the more I dug into the metaphor, the more connections I could find between the two ideas… both are interested in creating something that is compelling *now,* that will remain relevant into the future. Both require a great deal of research and engagement with the client, who ultimately 'receives' the finished product. Both require a great deal of vision and imagination. Both require the ability to see things differently from others.

Take something and try to improve upon it. Your toaster annoys you? How would you design it to resolve the things that bother you? You don't like the way that coffee mug feels in your hand? Why not? What's different about it compared with coffee mugs you *do* like?

Design problems are all around you: learn about, and invest some time in, thinking like a designer.

Feelings and Emotions

Get in touch with your feelings and emotions, you need to understand them, and you need to be able to evaluate them, and extract their value to propel you forward. This is hard, and not something that most people ever learn to do. Your emotions are chemical reactions inside your brain, triggered by certain things – memories, events, people, places.

For me, mindfulness is the key to leveraging my emotional state, and exerting some control over it, rather than it controlling me.

Memories

Your memories can be a great source of inspiration – both your happy memories, and your less happy memories. Just remember to be careful with your memories when you handle them. They can be altered by the act of recalling them.

Desires

What is it that you desire? Do you even know? A lot of people don't know. Or don't want to know. These are the people who will create a life story that enables a long run version of their status quo. "No, this is all I wanted" they say. "I work, I provide for my family, I spend time with my friends on the weekends, that's all I wanted". And maybe it is. But this story is also a safe way to define your lived existence to avoid sensing the gap... because sensing the gap between where you are and where you want to be can be painful and frustrating if you don't believe you possess the means and intention to make it happen.

So ask yourself, what do you desire? What are you prepared to do to achieve it?

Pain

Most people experience pain in their lives at some stage. The emotional pain that stems from the death of a loved one, the physical pain of an illness or injury. And sometimes it's both. Being bullied, for example, can cause both physical and emotional pain.

Physical pain is a rather unusual human state, in some regards, because you can't remember how it feels once it's gone. When you're in pain, it seems like you'll never feel any different – that this is as good as it gets, but then one day, you realise the pain is gone, and that you hadn't really noticed it going...

The human motivation to avoid pain is strong and compelling. If you have had experience of pain, you can draw on this motivation to propel you forward. It can be a great source of inspiration.

Observation

Some people are more observant than others. Have you noticed that? Sometimes it's the ability to spot change, say in the physical environment. Like a new shop popping up, or a new piece of public art, or a new paint scheme at a friend's house. Some people are observant of people, and notice the emotional state of others more readily. Some people have an eye for detail, and can recall with startling clarity events and individual component pieces of a situation that most people miss, or at least don't remember. The ability not just to see but to actually *observe* what is around you can be a tremendous source of inspiration.

The great news is that being observant is something you can practise if you put your mind to it. Police detectives and FBI agents aren't born with extraordinary observational powers, it is something that they are taught through their training, and that they hone through their practice. And you can too.

Mindfulness helps with this. The ability to quiet your mental chatter and spend your mental focus on something external rather than internal. The human brain is very poor at multitasking, so if you spend your walk to work busily preparing for a meeting you have at 9.00 am or ruing the unproductive discussion you had with a co-worker yesterday, you probably aren't attending to what is directly in front of you as you walk. So practice mentally describing to yourself what you see. The shadows, the colours, the advertising, the people, the wildlife, the signs of human habitation, the municipal workers, the facial expressions of people walking towards you. Pay attention, too, to how these things make you feel. Are you saddened by the homeless man proffering his hat and asking for change – or does it make you angry or uncomfortable? Did you know that your local performing arts society had a new play on next week? Do you know someone you think would like to know about that? Try and commit that detail to memory so you can tell them later.

Practising observing the world around you is a useful skill in many facets of your life, but can also be inspiring. Why is homelessness increasing in your town? Do amateur theatre companies promote themselves well enough? Live with these questions and you might be surprised where they take you and how they inspire you.

Question the Status Quo

Some people seem to be quite contrarian, and challenge everything. It can be a pain if it's directed at you... Have you ever had a family member, or a colleague who behaves as though they know the best way to do everything? I'm not talking about that kind of challenging. I'm talking about a kind of internal restlessness.

We have it as children. My four-year-old son, for example. It seems that 'why' is every third or fourth word that comes from his mouth at the moment. This innate curiosity is a wonderful gift. Because it is how we learn about the world around us. We start to build understanding. Why does that go with this? Why do these things happen this way?

But when you've heard "because I say so" often enough, you eventually stop asking. There's an important lesson here for the parents among us, but just because you've stopped asking, doesn't mean you can't *start* asking again.

Why do we do it this way? Why do we keep repeating this process that annoys our customers? Why do we complete that form when it *seems* as though nobody pays attention to it? Why do we provide this support to homeless people, but not actually solve the causes of their homelessness? Why do so many people dislike their jobs?

In some respects, this section could have been called *curiosity*. That's exactly what I'm talking about here. Being curious. Not making assumptions, instead asking questions. Particularly 'why'. Why is a phenomenally powerful word. I love it.

OK, I don't always love it – by the fifth time I've tried to explain to my four-year-old why we don't have ice cream for breakfast, I'm a little less enamoured of it, but *generally* I love it.

And the nice thing is, you can start really small with this one. You could set yourself a challenge to ask one 'why' question every day. Just a gentle one, even. Like: why do I put my socks on before my jeans? Answer: Because bootlegs weren't in fashion when I created my getting dressed habit, so for a while there, getting your socks on after your jeans were on was a bit more challenging... See – that wasn't so hard!

Wanting a Better Tomorrow

If you have children, you may understand what I'm about to say. Having a child made me an emotional wreck. And I don't mean in any clinical way – I am very grateful I didn't experience postpartum depression, or any of the very real and very difficult conditions that can stem from having a baby. I simply mean that I realised that my experience of love to that point had been two-dimensional compared with the love I felt for that odd little munched up bundle of arms and legs. I still haven't completely recovered my ability to watch the news on television. I cannot read about bad things happening to kids – particularly those of a similar age to my son. If I do, I cry. And I hurt inside. So generally I avoid it.

I also have no desire to exclude these things completely from my consciousness, because that would be artificial and false. So the challenge is, what can I *do* about it.

Take child abuse. For every horrific and tragic death you see or read about in the news media, there are hundreds – if not thousands of equally tragic cases that haven't quite ended in the same outcome, but are harmful and life-altering for those kids. So using what I know about the power of questions, I ask myself what could be done about it. What could I do about it. How could the system be better equipped to identify these situations and prevent them from escalating.

But more than that. I ask myself how could you prevent it from happening in the first place. What would it take to create a world where all children were born into families that loved them, to parents with the emotional control and communication skills required to deal with life's frustrations and setbacks without lashing out.

I want to find ways to counter-intuitively fix the problem. Governments are struggling, globally, to come up with workable and meaningful solutions. So I'm going to keep asking the questions. I don't think domestic violence is an immutable fact of life. I think it is a by-product of something going wrong that could go right. So I'm going to keep asking. And I'm going to keep trying to inspire others to ask as well. Because the more people ask these questions, the more clever, motivated, intentional people searching for answers, the more likely we are to come up with potential solutions.

Spotlight: Meditation And Mindfulness

"Meditation is to be aware of every thought and of every feeling, never to say it is right or wrong, but just to watch it and move with it. In that watching, you begin to understand the whole movement of thought and feeling. And out of this awareness comes silence." Jiddu Krishnamurti

I've referred to mindfulness a couple of times now, so I thought it might be useful to just be clear about what I mean. Mindfulness is a skill – and you develop it in the same way you would any other fine motor skill – by practising.

Summon an image of somebody meditating to mind. What did you think of?

Probably somebody sitting cross-legged in lotus pose, palms upwards, saying "ommmm", right? Or Buddha.

I'd encourage you to think of meditation more like mental exercise. You know if you want to strengthen your core muscles you need to workout, right? The same is true for your mind.

Meditation is a structured way to exercise your mind – strengthening its ability to 'observe' itself, thereby reducing the frequency with which you experience the 'amygdala-hijack' when your emotional brain takes over and makes decisions for you.

When you practice meditation regularly, you will find you become more mindful – that is, more aware of the present moment, what you are thinking about, and how you are feeling. And importantly, that these thoughts and feelings are just thoughts and feelings – they aren't 'you'.

Concluding Thoughts About Inspiration

"I decided that it was not wisdom that enabled poets
to write their poetry, but a kind of instinct or
inspiration, such as you find in seers and prophets
who deliver all their sublime messages without
knowing in the least what they mean." Socrates

Inspiration is the foundation of this journey. If you aren't inspired, you can expect a life of sitting on the couch watching reruns of *Everybody Loves Raymond*.

That doesn't mean your life won't be full and feel significant to you. I'm not making any judgments about what you choose to do with your life. But if you picked up this book because you're looking for something more… it all starts with inspiration.

Inspiration usually starts as something external – something out in the world. Your job is to *internalise* it. You have to bring it inside you. You have to connect it with who you are and the experiences and memories that define you. Otherwise, it will remain something out there, and your motivation to do something about it will remain idle.

I wrote this book because I don't have all the answers. If I had all the answers, I'd just head out into the world and start fixing all the things I can see myself. That would be super inspiring and intentional and impactful. But I have supreme confidence that somebody, somewhere, is going to come up with simple, elegant solutions to some of the world's problems that will be completely different to anything I would come up with. Better still, I know that some of you are going to solve problems that I don't even know exist. How awesome is that!

A care package for the planet that gets us all back on an even keel. Or a nanoparticle that consumes carbon dioxide from the atmosphere and returns it to the earth. A training package for first-time parents that's super cheap to deliver and builds resilience and communication skills so that parents are better equipped to handle the inevitable ups and downs of raising kids without resorting to violence. The democratisation of healthcare. The tools to feed everyone on the planet without destroying it. The marketing campaign that persuades people not to harvest white rhino horns or elephant tusks. The device that collects and breaks-down plastics safely so they don't kill sea-life. The therapy that prevents Alzheimer's Disease or cures cancer.

Whatever it is that makes you cross or angry or determined… that. That's what you can do. Don't worry if you don't know how. Nobody knows how until they have. Don't worry if you don't have a team to help you. Nobody does until they start building one. Don't worry if you don't have the money. Nobody does, until they start asking for it.

We start our lives as idealists – in the main. We believe we can do anything, be anything, achieve anything we set our minds to, until somebody – usually very well-meaning, a parent or a teacher – starts telling us we can't. Or we shouldn't. To be more *realistic*.

But now, if you've worked through the exercises in this section, you should be feeling a stirring – the beginnings of an inspired journey. An itch to get started. And maybe a little bit of fear as well. A little bit of self-doubt. That's good. It means you're on to something. Don't let that stop you. You haven't really done anything yet, and it certainly isn't anything scary or dangerous! You've written some words and talked to somebody about your memories… No sabre-tooth tigers.

But hopefully you can now understand why we start with inspiration. It's an incredibly important motivator. Some of it comes from within you – things you've already experienced and learned. But you also need to feed it. You need to maintain its potency by adding to it. By fuelling it. By seeking out sources of inspiration – positive and negative, big and small – around you every day and putting this into the engine. You wouldn't buy a brand new Tesla and then never plug it in, would you?

You need the engine *and* the fuel to make it run. And that fuel does get used up, so you need to replenish it.

And most importantly, you need to learn and believe that inspiration isn't some flighty thing that may or may not happen on any given day, but that it is something you have control over. You just need to choose it. You need to seek it out. You need to want it and look for it.

The rest is just implementation…

Part Two: Overcoming Indecision 🦋

3. The Power Of Decision

"A human being is a deciding being." Viktor E. Frankl

Congratulations! You're inspired! Now what?

I'm glad you asked.

Now you have to *decide*.

You have to decide you're going to do something. Something different than what you've been doing until this point. Something you might not have done before. Something you maybe don't know how to do. Something you don't even know *can* be done.

Have you ever known somebody who was a smoker? Who wanted to give up smoking? Many people believe it is willpower that helps you quit a habit like smoking. It isn't. You have to actually *decide* that you will quit smoking. Not "I'll try". Not "I'll give up in the New Year". Not "tomorrow". You have to *decide* so convincingly that *you* believe you. Because once you decide, you're no longer a smoker.

But you have to *believe* you've decided. If your brain is still using the word 'try' even if you're saying out loud to friends and colleagues "I'm giving up" it won't work. In fact "I'm giving up" is still a future tense statement – loosely translated it says to your brain "I'm going to, but I haven't yet".

The same is true of many things. Exercising more. Eating less. Spending more time at home. Drinking less. Saving money. Creating a business.

Please don't misunderstand me. I'm not saying that making a decision is easy. And I'm not saying that, even once you make up your mind to do it, that there aren't moments when you wonder about whether you made the *right* decision. But if you have *actually* decided, and your brain believes you, then your brain starts lining up your subsequent decisions and behaviours to match that decision.

As soon as being a non-smoker becomes your identity, your brain will go out of its way to remain consistent to that identity. After all, it's who you are!

So in this section, I'm going to show you the things that need to be in place to actually – convincingly and finally – reach a decision that your brain believes:

- Clarity
- Conviction
- Consistency, and
- Confirmation

But before we do that, a little recap on the way your brain works, so that you know what you're in for. Forewarned is forearmed, as they say.

Your brain loves being comfortable. Warm, full, content. Safe. There's a reason they call it the comfort zone. It's full of all the things you know and love. Routine. Consistency. Predictability.

By definition, doing something new takes you outside your comfort zone. And let's face it – the thing you're now inspired to do is *way* outside your comfort zone. Otherwise you would have done it already!

Your brain wants to keep you safe. It wants to survive. It worries about you. It genuinely believes that the path of least resistance is the surest way to living a long, healthy (and reproductive) life.

Is this system useful? Sure!

Is it perfect? Not by a long shot.

Your brain frequently chooses to eat highly calorific food, even when it's low in nutritional value, just in case you encounter a famine... or need to run five miles to escape a sabre-tooth tiger[*]. Which obviously is highly unlikely...

Your brain prevents you from doing things that *seem* inherently risky but could have significant benefits to you in terms of your well-being – like delivering that killer presentation that gets you promoted.

Your brain despises physical exercise if it doesn't serve an actual purpose, like escaping from a... you get the point. Your brain

[*] Don't say I didn't warn you about sabre-tooth tigers.

equates comfort with safety, and discomfort with danger. Without providing you much by way of grey areas in between.

I'm sharing this with you because everything we've done up until now has been mental work. We've been dreaming, imagining, talking, planning, thinking. But we're about to start getting real. We're about to get concrete. We're about to put some wheels in motion. So expect to get uncomfortable.

But perhaps more importantly, expect your brain to start telling you things that cast doubt. That make you wonder if you're wasting your time. Or whether you're even entitled to be working on this big amazing thing you're inspired to do. I mean who are you to save the world?

This usually comes in the form of 'what-if' statements. What if I fail? What if nobody likes it? What if nobody agrees with me? What if it doesn't work? What if...?

And your brain is sneaky. It knows exactly how to hit you where it hurts. If you care about financial security: what if you lose your job? If you are a doting parent: what if your kids miss out on something? If you lack confidence: what if you embarrass yourself? Talk about low-blows!

But your brain doesn't have to play fair. The stakes are life and death! It has your actual survival in mind. You should be grateful!

So what do you do to express gratitude? You say thank you.

That's all. You say thank you.

Thank you for worrying, but I got this.

Recognise this voice as your inner critic – even give it a name if that helps (something that makes it seem silly works well – like Ethel or Nigel[*]). I first came across this idea in Tara Mohr's brilliant book *Playing Big*. I've found it hugely helpful in tackling some of the bigger challenges in my own life.

So once again, with feeling…

"Thanks for worrying about me Nigel, but I've got this".

Making A Decision Your Brain Believes

So let's take a look at the features of a decision that Nigel will take seriously.

Clarity

The very first thing you need to do is be very clear about what the decision is you want to make. It should be written down somewhere, even if it's just in your journal, or on a scrap of paper.

Some decisions are easier to clarify than others, in terms of specificity. This is like setting SMART goals, but a little more flexible.

Make sure you start with "I have decided". See how this is past tense? It sounds like you've already done it.

I'll show you some examples:

- *I have decided* to give up smoking
- *I have decided* to write a book that helps people change the world

---

[*] Nigel is a major character in this book. He's my inner critic. He's my procrastination monkey. He's my maintainer of the status quo. His intentions are good – he wants to keep me safe. He's just not very up-to-date with the 21st century world I live in. I feel affection for him. Like an ageing great-uncle who hardly gets out and always causes a scene at Christmas…

- *I have decided* to lose ten kilograms
- *I have decided* to take up a leadership role in my company
- *I have decided* to improve the quality of my marriage
- *I have decided* to live a life of intent and impact

Do you notice that none of them explain *how* you're going to do this thing. That's OK. How comes later. This is the 'what'.

Conviction

After you know what the decision is, you need to want it. And I mean *really* want it. This comes from your 'why'. Your inspiration. You need to connect your why with your what.

I have decided to give up smoking, because I want to live long enough to see my grandchildren grow up.

I have decided to write a book that helps people change the world because I believe that everyone has greatness within them, and that I can help them achieve that greatness.

I have decided to live a life of intent and impact, because I want to contribute to making the world a better place, and I don't want to die thinking I left anything on the table.

This is the bigger, higher purpose behind your decision. This is what you will need to focus on when the going gets tough, and Nigel is telling you to stop. This is the place where, if you are religious or spiritual, you can bring in this calling or higher power that guides you.

Consistency

In his book *The Speed of Trust,* Steven Covey Jr. outlines the things that character witnesses must demonstrate in a court of law in order to be 'trusted' by the judge or jury making the decision in the case, or at least that their lawyers must demonstrate on their behalf. He breaks it into four areas, one of which is **results**, or track record. In other words, does this individual have a history of achievement in this area – the area they are being asked to speak about. For example, if the witness is an expert in some area of science – or even law – have they published? Are they regarded an expert in this field by 'verifiable others'. Other scientists, other lawyers. Does their employer (university or law firm) have a good reputation. Have they *consistently* been considered to know about this particular thing, and does their behaviour and track record back it up?

Now this intuitively makes sense – if we are deciding whether or not to believe someone, we want to know if the thing we are being asked to believe is a current fad or a long-standing view.

But it gets really interesting when it comes to asking this same question of yourself – which is what you are doing when you try to make a decision about something. Particularly when it is something that your brain is telling you is risky or uncomfortable.

The difference though, between observing this in a court of law and doing it inside your own head? There's no lawyer to play the role of 'for' and 'against'. There's no prosecution and no defence to speak of – just you. And Nigel.

So you may not even be consciously aware that this battle is raging inside your head. And Nigel is pretty good at being insidious about it, he'll have you believing his side of things in no time if you don't pay attention!

So let's use the example of giving up smoking for a minute. It's conceptually simple, but actually very hard.

In order to convince your brain that you are serious, like really serious, about giving up smoking, you need to take some small actions, that are aligned.

Stop buying cigarettes. People who don't smoke don't buy cigarettes. Get rid of any ashtrays in the house. People who don't smoke don't generally like people smoking in their house, so get rid of them. Make a commitment towards helping you quit smoking, like joining a support group. And subscribing to an anti-smoking therapy, like nicotine patches or another physical support mechanism. But be really clear that this is temporary, you won't need it soon.

Identify an alternative habit that you are happy with... A lot of people worry that when they give up smoking they will put on weight, because they will eat more in the times when they would have had a cigarette. It can ideally be something really positive. Like writing, or a brisk walk, or something like that. Chewing gum might work – it needs to be something that makes sense to you.

There should be more than this – you need to create some time in your schedule to sit down and think about the things that people who *don't* smoke do or don't do that you can imitate.

But – and this is a big but – you also need to create some supporting habits at the same time. Particularly if you believe you are somebody who doesn't 'stick at things'. For example if you've tried five times in the past to give up smoking, without success, your brain will quite happily tell you that you have no track-record in giving up smoking. In fact you have an extensive track record of *not* giving up smoking. So what makes you think you're suddenly different?

So a supporting habit might be something completely unrelated to smoking, but that you know you can do, and stick to, so that when the negative voice creeps in saying 'you can't do this' you can answer – I'm great at creating positive habits – look how I've successfully gone to bed 10 minutes earlier than usual every day for the past week – I can set and maintain positive habits.

And hold on to the fact that when you do successfully quit smoking, you will have a real humdinger of a positive track record to point to for *new* challenges that your brain tries to talk you out of… "of course I can train to run a half marathon – I quit smoking, remember!"

Confirmation

When you think, you tend to think in words. (Quietly inside your head, obviously.)

These words are not always obvious, but you hear them even if you aren't intentionally listening. Usually, your internal chatter (Nigel, but others as well) will be confirming and justifying your current behaviour.

- "But I have an addictive personality, so smoking is just part of who I am" (No it isn't!)
- "I've always been a smoker" (No you haven't!)

- "I have the most fun outside with the smokers at parties" (how do you know what you were missing out on inside?)

All of this chatter, whether you actually hear it or not, weakens your resolve. So you must replace it with new chatter. These are what are typically referred to as 'affirmations'. But if you have a negative reaction to that word, let me explain.

There is nothing magical or fluffy about affirmations. They can't manifest abundance out of thin air. They don't suddenly give you magical powers. They can't help you win the lottery.

What they can do, is drown out the negative self-talk so that you can't hear it. And, when you brain hears something often enough, even if initially it doesn't agree, eventually you change its mind (or your mind, I guess).

So develop two or three statements that you memorise, and say internally (or out loud) often enough that it starts to drown out the chatter.

When your colleague comes and asks you to go for a cigarette, say "I'm not a smoker". *Don't say* "I'm trying to give up".

When you feel the urge to go outside for a cigarette: "I don't smoke" – out loud if you can, but internally if it's not an appropriate situation.

Say it out loud five times when you wake up in the morning. Write it down where you can read it regularly. Say it to yourself as you go to bed at night… when you brush your teeth… when you buy the groceries.

If you say it often enough, you'll start to believe it's true, and then, it is true!

So what does all this have to do with overcoming indecision? What I've outlined here are the four things you need to do in order to *actually* decide to do something different than what you ordinarily would:

- You need clarity – what is it you are deciding
- You need conviction – why does this matter to you
- You need consistency – build a track-record that belongs to the sort of person who already does this thing, create new habits to replace old ones
- You need confirmation – keep telling yourself – literally telling yourself – that you've already done the thing, or that you are the person who can do the thing

I promise, you'll be amazed at what you can accomplish once you actually **decide**.

4. Inspiration Is Great But...

By now, you're feeling inspired, you know your 'why' and you've decided you're going to do something about it. Something significant.

We're about to kick on into phase two, Intent, but they say that forewarned is forearmed – so let's take a quick look at some of the things that might crop up. I want to talk about the things that might derail you, even before you get started...

The idea here is that you can be prepared... you can recognise them for what they are and prevent them from throwing you off course.

Failure Of Courage And Confidence

"You gain strength, courage, and confidence by every experience in which you really stop to look fear in the face. You are able to say to yourself, 'I lived through this horror. I can take the next thing that comes along." Eleanor Roosevelt

In many respects, courage and confidence are two sides of the same coin. If you are feeling confident, the chances are you will not need courage per se. But if your confidence drops, you'll need courage to come to the fore and get you over that hump.

So what is confidence, really...

Do you remember in the last chapter we talked about results and track-record? When you've already done something – you've done it before – confidence is relatively easy. But as soon as you start working on a variation to that previous experience, say you want to go bigger, or better, or faster, or further, or longer… whatever it is that is different will push your brain into that 'Argh! Change! Freak out!" space we referred to. Nigel feels obliged to keep you safe – even if it's keeping you safe from yourself.

Courage, on the other hand, is doing something *even when* you are afraid and lack confidence. Make no mistake – courage is not the absence of fear, it's the ability to do it anyway, in spite of your fear.

Remember the trick of thanking Nigel – or whatever you decide to call your inner critic – thanking Nigel. He's trying to take care of you. It's just that he can't see the whole picture in the way you can. He just knows you're afraid and wants to keep you safe. So thank him, let him know you're OK, and plow on regardless. You got this.

One final note on confidence and your inner critic. I mentioned in the previous section that Nigel knows exactly what buttons to push to turn you into a quivering indecisive wreck…

But sometimes he's far more insidious. Don't be surprised if he moves on to what *appear* to be more 'factual' or concrete things. Like: "you're not qualified to do this – you should go back to university first" or "if this was actually worth doing, somebody would already have done it"…

Just remember this. The fact that you were able to conceptualise this thing means you are uniquely qualified to do it. Do you need to know everything? No! And who are you trying to prove your legitimacy to? If you need to be a lawyer to tackle the issue you're trying to solve, then Nigel might have a point, but if you can get a lawyer on your team and be just as effective, then tell him to go away. (I mean, thank him!)

And as for 'somebody would already be doing this if it was worth doing'… its simply not true. Your unique experiences, and viewpoints and place in the world may allow you to see things in a way that nobody else can. And besides, all progress in the world – all of it – happened when somebody challenged the status quo for the first time. Every major invention was, in fact, an invention. By definition, something done for the first time. First times are good. And even if you discover somebody is already trying to do the same thing as you, take that as confirmation that you are on the right track.

Failure Of Optimism And Hope

"Positive thinking is the notion that if you think good thoughts, things will work out well. Optimism is the feeling of thinking things will be well and be hopeful." Martin Seligman

Nobody is optimistic all the time. There are plenty of circumstances in the world that can make you despair. People do silly things. Mean things even. There is violence, and hatred, and bigotry. It can be easy, when faced with these things, to slip into a sense of helplessness. How can you – one person – make a difference when the scale of the problem is so big, so ingrained?

The answer – as with most things – is one step at a time!

By the way, that sense of pessimism and despair – that's another one of Nigel's voices. He's feeling you sense the scale of the job, and he's protecting you from disappointment. You know what to do… "Thank you Nigel."

I'm not suggesting that you can – or even should – be optimistic all the time. And even when you are feeling optimistic, this shouldn't be a Pollyanna-ish naiveté – it needs to be tinged with scepticism, otherwise you'll be constantly disappointed and/or surprised by what the world deals up in response to what you are doing.

Failure Of Consistency And Persistence

"Energy and persistence conquer all things."
Benjamin Franklin

You will make mistakes along the way. Some of them will be small, but some of them may be big. There is absolutely no shame in making mistakes – it shows you are trying. Which most people aren't. You might be embarrassed, or ashamed of the mistake. Don't be. That's Nigel again. He senses your emotional response to making a mistake – whatever it is – and wants to protect you from it.

Our prehistoric forebears relied heavily on each other for survival. Particularly women, who were often responsible for caring for children, or were pregnant. The fledgling origins of our modern social networks were vital for survival – specialisation of labour meant that it was very hard for one person to survive on their own for very long. There was safety in numbers. Being ostracised could be a death sentence.

So Nigel evolved mechanisms for protecting you from social embarrassment, from shame, from 'standing out' for any reason that might not be helpful to the clan. So he's sensing these emotions and worried that you're going to get left behind, and left to fend for yourself.

"Thank you Nigel, I got this."

The challenge, then, is not to avoid mistakes, but to make them often, and quickly. And to reflect on those mistakes *only for the purpose of learning*, and then to try again. The saying "get straight back on the horse" is relevant here. You need to persist, otherwise, the larger the gap between the mistake happening and you trying again, the more time Nigel has to persuade you not to bother.

If this is something that interests you, you should read *Grit* by Angela Duckworth. In it, she outlines the reasons why grit is critical to achieving success in any field that is difficult. Drawing on a significant body of research, she has isolated Grit as one of the key factors that is most correlated with success in any discipline – more so than raw talent, passion, inspiration, or practice alone.

Failure Of Creativity

> *"Creativity is putting your imagination to work, and it's produced the most extraordinary results in human culture."* Ken Robinson

What if I run out of ideas? What if I'm not creative enough to figure out the next steps when my first attempt doesn't succeed? Welcome back Nigel! The same things that we talked about in the previous section on inspiration should help you here. Go somewhere new. Talk to someone about what you're struggling with. Visit a favourite place. Meditate. Get into nature. Walk barefoot in the grass.

There are lots of *things* you can do when you feel uninspired that may help. Sometimes a simple change of scene – or even a good night's sleep – is all it takes.

Creativity is never finite though. Remember this. It's important. There is always more. And it can show up in the strangest ways, at the strangest times.

Also, there are tactics you can deploy. This next example is dear to my heart right now.

I'm writing this book for you early in the mornings. I have a busy day job, a four-year-old and a blog. The only time available for me to write this book, which I genuinely believe can change the world, is between 5.45 am and 6.30 am every morning.

Now you might have heard of the idea of writer's block? The abject failure to think of anything to write? Imagine waking up in the morning, grabbing a cup of coffee (essential to writing *anything at all*) and then sitting down in front of a blank screen... I can hear Nigel getting excited right now, even just as I'm describing this!

Knowing all of this, I don't allow the blank screen... I have planned this book out in quite a bit of detail – I have an outline that includes what the chapters are called, and the broad concepts that will be in each section. So I know, the night before, what I'm going to be writing about the next morning.

In addition, I make some little rules for myself...

- It's about quantity, not quality. I can fix quality later
- It's not creativity – it's work. This is a little mind trick. Of course I'm being creative, but I'm not relying on some flash of insight to get started – I can come back and be 'clever and creative' later
- No research. (Nigel loves telling me that I should check this, or look up that, or find out a bit more about something.   Who are you to write about that? He says...)
- No breaks, no social media, no interruptions. In 45 minutes I can write 1,500 words. If I do this consistently every day, a 75,000 word book will take me 50 days to write. Fifty. That's hardly anything. Ten weeks if I only write on weekdays.

Thanks Nigel. I got this.

Remember, your brain – presuming it has your best interests, even your survival, at heart – is trying to do what it thinks is right for you. Persuading you to maintain the status quo. Persuading you that this is going to be painful, and scary, and dangerous, and embarrassing, and possibly fatal. But you have access to your frontal cortex – an altogether more sophisticated piece of bio-tech that can logically assess these risks.

Thanks Nigel, I got this.

Part Three: Intent 🦋

5. Introducing Intent

"Our intention creates our reality." Wayne Dyer

So you're feeling inspired, you've decided you're going to do something about it... now what?

The next thing you need to do is clearly and concisely set your intent. So in this section we'll learn a bit about what intent is, how to set it, and what tools and techniques will be useful to you in capturing your intent, and clarifying what that may mean or require in the future.

Why Does Intent Matter?

Have you ever found yourself in an argument with your significant other because something you did upset them, but although you're now just as grumpy as they are, that wasn't your intent? Or have you got partway through a project or task and realised it isn't turning out quite the way you intended?

Intent matters. This is your centering position – it's what you measure your success against. If you don't document it from the outset, you'll never know whether you've achieved the goals you set, or not. It's also a brilliant guide for decision-making. Being crystal clear about what you *intend* to happen means that you can make adjustments and course corrections along the way if your actions aren't taking you in the right direction.

One of the most stressful and challenging roles I've had in my career has been picking up the pieces after a very, very bad IT service implementation. The service, catastrophically, was a payroll system responsible for paying upwards of 100,000 people every fortnight. And to make matters worse, these people were teachers, principals and support staff in public schools.

Needless to say, when people started not being paid, or being paid incorrectly, things got heated quickly. And fair enough! Nobody should be paid incorrectly for work they've done – it's a basic fundamental of employment.

I was employed by the organisation that had procured the system: chosen the vendor and set the specification for the service to be delivered. A lot of fingers were being pointed in our direction, very fast. In fact, for quite a while when things started going wrong, most people didn't even know the name of the vendor.

The responsibility of media spokesperson fell to me, and within a few weeks of the system going 'live' I was fronting television and radio interviews where I was being asked entirely legitimate questions about how this could have happened – or been allowed to happen.

Very early on when this started I sat down and wrote out a few lines on a piece of paper:

- I didn't choose the vendor
- The most important thing is to get people paid correctly, as quickly as possible
- People are allowed to feel angry/annoyed/frustrated if they aren't being paid correctly
- The situation is indefensible – so don't defend it
- Focus on recognising the significance of the impact on real people
- Focus on getting it fixed

Now this is a pretty short list. It's not technical at all. There's no jargon, there's no explanation of what's actually going wrong. In fact, to be honest, at the point I wrote this, nobody even knew what *was* going wrong or why it was happening.

But this simple list helped me clarify exactly how to approach every interview. I didn't get riled up when some people took advantage of the situation to get in a dig about something else entirely. I didn't blame the vendor. I accepted responsibility for fixing the situation. I focused on explaining how people could get their pay fixed. There were other avenues for working with sector leaders on the knock-on impacts for schools and communities – but national news media wasn't the place for that.

The impact of this clarity was twofold: it minimised the preparation time I needed to do before each interview (which meant more time focused on fixing things, and driving our team towards correcting the system) and it meant that when I was interviewed I was able to answer questions in a calm, clear, unflustered way – even the most curly ones!

Having a very clear intent is important. It's not the whole puzzle, but it's a vital piece.

What Is Intent?

At its simplest, intent is a clear statement of purpose. What am I trying to do? It's future oriented, and if your inspiration is stemming from a gap you've recognised between what is and what could be, it's focused on improving something. Making something better than it was before.

Another characteristic of intent, which I find helpful, is that it can recognise that the pathway is unclear and that the final destination may change along the way. But it does – and must – set a direction of travel. And there's a degree to which that direction of travel needs to be based on something concrete.

In an organisation, this statement of intent might be referred to as a mission statement or a purpose. As an individual, though, it might not be all of your 'why', but it's definitely a piece of the why.

What Is My Intent?

I'll give you an example. My 'why' is to help people lead inspired, intentional, impactful lives, so that together we can resolve the world's broken pieces. My intent right now is to write this book, because I know that this book, for some people, will be the exact impetus they need to get up and do something positive in the world.

But I don't for a minute think that I achieve my why by writing and publishing just one book. In many regards, I see the book as the first step in my 'why' journey. The platform from which other projects and activities will be based.

However, the book provides me an opportunity to share the genesis of my thinking. It allows me to test how people will respond to my life's purpose, in terms of whether it is translatable. My intent is to enable you to change your life, and the lives of those around you so that suffering and pain is reduced, and a sense of purpose and accomplishment – however *you* define that – is enhanced.

I have a logic train – a series of 'if-then' statements that make me sufficiently confident that this book is a useful stepping stone in that journey. But I don't know if that's true. I probably shouldn't admit that – it's not a great way to sell books! But I'm also not aware of anyone trying to do something like this before… It's a bit on the audacious side, after all. Who really believes they can fix the world? (Thanks Nigel, I got this.)

What Will You Find In This Section?

In the remainder of this section, we'll talk about three complementary approaches to setting intent that should be of assistance to you. Please don't view them as either/or… they are both/and (or whatever the 'three things' equivalent of 'both' is).

The first is **strategic thinking**. Strategic thinking is about finding ways to reduce the uncertainty you have about the future. There's no point over-egging this – the future is unknowable. But there are a number of strategies that can reduce that uncertainty, and, perhaps more importantly, highlight where the opportunities are for you to *influence* that future, thereby increasing the likelihood that your intent will create impact.

The second is **research**. This is a tricky one, because Nigel likes research. Research is not dangerous. Research is safe. Research also has a tendency to identify dozens of reasons that Nigel can use to persuade you this is a terrible idea. So this approach comes with a definite cautionary note... There's a sweet spot for research. Extend past that sweet spot at the peril of your entire inspiring intent...

The third is **planning and goal setting**. Most people will be somewhat familiar with this, but we're going to spend a bit of time talking about why it works, what the science behind it is, and how to get to the meatiest goals – the ones that are really going to propel you forward – as quickly as possible.

So let's get started!

6. Strategic Thinking

"Strategy is about making choices, trade-offs; it's about deliberately choosing to be different." Michael Porter

One of the real challenges with setting goals – particularly traditional SMART goals[*] that are specific, measurable and so forth – is that while you can set the goals, and quantify as much as you can about what they are and how you'll accomplish them, and by when... your actions towards those goals occur within a world that includes things over which you have very little control.

Generally I have observed that people are great at saying "in five years I will be a millionaire" and then setting actions and plans for the next few months... but the gap between the end of the period for which people feel sufficiently certain to *plan for* and the period people *wish* to achieve their big hairy audacious goal is significant, uncertain and full of fluffiness. In case you're wondering, goal setting and fluffiness don't mix well.

So how can you reduce the uncertainty you have about the things that you can't control?

There's an entire discipline of thought built around this very question, and it's called strategy.

Before we get started on finding out what this is all about, though, a cautionary note...

---

[*] By the way, I have no problem with SMART goals, but I think they leave some important components out... we'll meet a modified version of SMART goals in Chapter 8.

Strategic thinking tools can be a lot of fun and Nigel likes them... a lot. Because while you are busy identifying potential variables in an uncertain future, you are doing two things: you aren't taking any actual action **and** you are providing Nigel with material. You hopefully know him well enough now to know that he is constantly on the lookout for ammunition to use against you when you stand poised for action. In that moment where you hesitate... "but what if there's a change of government?" or "what if the economy tanks?" or "what if the regulatory environment for electric vehicles changes substantially?" he's waiting to pounce.

Knowing this – and more importantly, knowing Nigel – I was in two minds whether to include this section in the book. Because, after all, the primary thing it does is give you greater clarity about all the ways your amazing exciting idea won't ever work...

Here's why I'm including it anyway.

Reason number one: If you work through these tools and you press on anyway, Nigel has no power over you. You will persist and you will succeed. That's amazing.

Reason number two: If you work through these tools and you press on anyway, not only does Nigel have no power over you, but when one of the things that you anticipated happens (even in a minor way, or slightly different than you anticipated) you will feel buoyed, because you anticipated it, planned for it, and know what to do. (See, Nigel? I got this!)

Reason number three: With practice, these tools gradually become ingrained in the way you think. This has a number of benefits, the most significant of which is that you gradually build confidence in your ability to troubleshoot and solve issues when they arise. You become less flustered by variations in the world outside your span of control, and much clearer about the areas you do control, and what to do differently as a consequence. This is so significant because eventually you will find that you don't feel the need to use these tools to make sense of the unknowable elements of the future anymore. You will accept there are a great number of things you don't control and you will back yourself to overcome them when they arise, rather than spending a lot of time anxious about what they might be and all the ways they might derail your plans.

Reason number four: Fun. Some of these tools are really fun – especially if you can work on them with someone else. And better still, when they are just for your edification, you don't need to worry too much about whether they are presented in a pretty way. You aren't likely to be sharing them widely, if at all. But the knowledge and the confidence that stems from working through the process is well worth the effort.

So what is strategy?

Well, there are nearly as many definitions as there are tools to create it, but the key points are:

- It is a methodology for increasing our knowledge of, or preparedness for, the future
- It is a methodology for creating a range of scenarios about likely futures

- It is an approach to the world that allows us to be clear about what we control, and what we don't control, and how we might influence the future options we've identified

- It helps us to understand where the points of influence are, when we have identified a preferred future scenario.

I know, this still sounds pretty fluffy. But don't worry, some of the tools for doing this are quite scientific – which is great for building confidence in the outcomes, but please never forget that what comes out can only be as good as what goes in.

If you do this work by yourself, the strategic futures scenarios that you invent can *only* be derived from what is already in your head. It really is a good idea to collect data and input from a range of sources, just to help you push past your own assumptions and biases. By the way, you can do this without telling anyone what you're working on, so don't stress too much about this. But equally, if you're working on this project with someone else, make sure they are involved too!

A Strategic Question

Strategic thinking has to start with a well defined strategic question. So what is a strategic question? For the purpose of this exercise, I'm going to rely heavily on the work of Geoff Coyle, author of *Practical Strategy: Structured Tools and Techniques*. In his book, Coyle explains that truly strategic problems are "so difficult, so very hard, that they cannot be handled using rigorous mathematics; only 'soft' approaches will get anywhere near coping with them". He goes on to outline 10 characteristics of strategic questions:

1. They address the very nature and fundamentals of the 'organisation' in question

2. There are likely to be numerous stakeholders or interested parties

3. They have imprecise objectives, that may be ambiguous or even conflicting

4. There is no 'right' answer to the problem

5. They have a long timeframe and long-term impact

6. They are so important that the answers cannot be left to chance – imaginative analysis is required

7. Because they are so complex, simplification into some form of model is required

8. They require structured thought and analysis to solve them – there cannot be a 'formula'

9. They likely need several different methodologies to get close to a workable solution or solutions – flexibility is key

10. There is no 'solution' only illuminating judgments that will give guidance about what to do

Figuring out this question is one of my favourite things about strategic thinking. It's not just any old question, but a question that you need the answer to. A question that is future-oriented. A question that will motivate you to keep going and that is connected with your inspiration – your 'why'.

I have a couple of examples for you.

One of my questions is "what would have to be true for child abuse to end in the developed world?"

Now please don't misunderstand this question: it isn't that I think child abuse is OK in other places. The reason I've narrowed the focus in this question is because it reduces the variables. You can have more than one strategic question. In this case, the reason this question is narrower is because there is an (untested) assumption that the causes of child abuse in the developed world may be different than the causes of child abuse in the developing world. Now the beauty of a good strategic question is that answering it will lead to insights into other related matters. If the causes of child abuse in the developed world are *related to* the developed world (massive wage disparity between the haves and have-nots, increased stress from lack of social support, displacement from one's family and community), then potentially the solutions lie in resolving those issues. However, if the exercise reveals that the causes are fundamentally human – not related to things specific to the developed world, then the solutions may be transferable. For example, lack of basic communication skills and the ability to self-regulate emotions. If you figure out how to resolve these root causes, you may be onto something that would work in other contexts. But if you ask the wrong question up front, you may not realise this straight away.

Another example of a great strategic question is "what skills do I need to learn, and/or help my kids develop, to prepare for an uncertain future in the employment market?"

This is a bit closer to home, I suspect, for most of us. It's focused on action now, but the 'uncertain world' part is what will require analysis. It adds a fairly specific timeframe insofar as you are interested in the working lifespan of you and/or your kids – whatever their age is now, plus the number of years you think they will be seeking employment.

What I also like about this question is that it forces you to look beyond specific industries or employers. What's driving the question is the nature of work in the future – not the nature of work now. When you have some ideas about the nature of future work, you will need to understand the gap between the current employment market and the future employment market. But I suspect that answering this question will inevitably take you down some paths you might not expect.

For example, you will inevitably explore AI and robotics. You will wonder about the social safety net that your government provides you (which could create an entirely new source of inspiration and advocacy for you). You will need to think about the value of qualifications. The nature of leisure. The value of money. It will take you in to some diverse but very relevant areas of exploration. And you may find that you ultimately end up less at a set of transferable skills for job-seekers, and more at either a set of human competencies (relationships, communication, imagination, problem-solving) OR a pet project that you think will improve the future of work nationally, or within your community. You might be inspired to create a community learning centre that focuses on helping people identify and develop skills on an individualised level. Or you might be inspired to develop a series of webinars or courses that focus on these skills and competencies.

Remember, the question needs to be future-oriented. It needs to be implausible that there is only one answer (technically you aren't actually looking for an answer – it's OK if it just creates more questions), and it has to be fundamentally impactful on the area you are inspired to take action in.

Take a minute to brainstorm some potential questions. Write them down. You don't have to choose one now. Live with it, refine it. And remember that you can refine it as you go, provided it doesn't cease to be a strategic question.

Strategic Tools For Unravelling Complexity: The "Why" Tree

In addition to having identified your own 'why' I want you to put the wonderful word 'why' to another use. If you have kids, you know how frustrating the repeated 'why?' can be. Particularly when it relates to going to bed. Or eating your vegetables. Asking it, repeatedly, is like a one hour set of wind-sprints for your brain.

Let's look at the first strategic question we explored above: "what would have to be true for child abuse to end in the developed world?"

First, this question needs to be reworded as a 'why' question: "why is there child abuse in the developed world?" Write this question in the top centre of a large blank page. Write down all the answers you can think of in a fan, splaying out below the original question.

Then ask 'whys' of all your answers. If one of your answers was "because parents lack oral communication skills", the question becomes "WHY do parents lack oral communication skills?". Again write all the answers branching out from this question...

If one of your answers was "because they didn't learn these skills from their parents or their schooling" why?

Keep repeating the process until you can't ask 'why' anymore, and repeat with all the answers to the original question. You'll end up with something that looks a bit like an upside down tree.

In my experience, it gets a bit hard to find more 'why' answers once you've gone down about six or seven layers. But by that point, you'll have some really exciting and interesting ideas for what causes the problem you're trying to solve *and* some ideas for how you might start to address the problems you've found.

Furthermore, and quite importantly, this process helps to shed light on how multi-causal and multi-faceted these big tricky problems are. Not every instance of child abuse will be caused or triggered by the same factors, and not every solution will work in every instance.

Now, perhaps frustratingly by this point, you sometimes find you need to repeat the process using one of your answers as a new strategic question. If you figured out that one of the points of intervention might be your local public schooling system, for example, you might need to ask why it isn't already happening – what are the conditions and circumstances in public schooling that would need to change in order that teachers were more likely to impart the communication skills and emotional self-regulation practices that might prevent today's kids becoming abusive parents? Do the teachers themselves have those skills? Do they have time to teach those skills? Are they expected to teach those skills? Do they know those skills are important?

The answers to each of these questions will likely result in a whole new line of thinking... A line of thinking that may reveal concrete actions you might take to accomplishing your own 'why'.

But don't stress too much about that now. For now, just focus on really broadening your own understanding of the issues at play. Almost all problems are more complex than we first think them to be. In your moments of frustration, when you find yourself saying "oh, if only they did [insert action here]" chances are that the individual in question has many more reasons why they don't do that thing than you have thought about.

Capture and keep your data somewhere you can come back to it...

Strategic Tools For Thinking About Possible Futures: Delphi Method

Another technique for identifying potential strategic future scenarios to inform intent is the Delphi Method. Named for the oracle at Delphi from Ancient Greece, the idea is that there is a font of wisdom out there, in the form of people who are experts in the topic in question.

Many of these experts care greatly about the topic and will happily share their thoughts with you via a short structured survey, along with a free-text question so that they can share their particular theory or point of view. You are really seeking their views on what they think will change in the field over a specific period of time – say 10 to 15 years. You're asking them to extrapolate from what they know and make some predictions. It is highly likely that you will need to promise anonymity to have much chance of getting a response.

You don't need too many of these, and you may find that they contradict each other. That's good. We've already talked about how if the answers to these questions were known, somebody would already have solved them! Don't worry too much if you don't get the answers back that you are expecting – or even any answers at all. Delphi is usually best for validating or invalidating existing assumptions. The chances are these experts are on the record already for some aspect of this topic – so you can analyse their existing material to reveal what you think they would have said.

Don't forget to include some wild-cards on your invite list. A robotics expert or computer programmer may have very different ideas about how things will impact on your strategic question in the future than, say, a psychologist or social worker.

You are really asking them to tell you a story about the future. And by analysing their responses, you, too, will have some understanding of what possible futures might exist.

Strategic Tools For Thinking About Possible Futures: Field Anomaly Relaxation (FAR)

The next technique is moderately more complex and involves a four-stage process. Ideally, it is done with a small team. It involves four discrete stages: visualising the future; developing effective language for the problem; testing for consistency; and forming scenarios.

Stage One: Visualise the Future

The first stage is to develop an imaginative view of the future into which your proposed intervention/s would unfold. Don't worry if you don't know what your interventions are yet! Just that you will have some. Imagine yourself out in the future – choose a timeframe that's relatively long-term but *also* relevant to your strategic question. If we stick with the ending child abuse question from earlier, you might want to think about 10 years, or 15. It's a big complex problem and it's likely to take a bit of unpicking. Chances are that within five years you'll just be getting started. Now write a short 'essay' of what the future will be like in the relevant domain. If you are working with others, it's a good idea to give each person a 'theme'. For example, one person should write a particularly optimistic essay – as though you've succeeded beyond your wildest dreams. Another should be asked to write a particularly gloomy scenario, where the problem has become much worse. And then a number of variants in-between.

Stage Two: Develop a Language for the Problem

Once you've settled on a time frame, take out a new blank sheet of paper (you can also use a mind-mapping app if you have one you like). Write your strategic question and the timeframe in the middle of the page. Thinking about all the essays that you've developed to visualise the future, you need to think about what the variables are between them. You're trying to identify environmental variables that you believe have an impact on your question, as shown by the various versions of the future. So, for example, you might have some obvious contenders: the state of the economy and employment market, education policy, you might have identified that the age of the mother at the birth of her first child has an impact. You might have identified rates of substance abuse as a factor. If you are looking at the problem from a global perspective, rather than just within your own jurisdiction, you might identify that the strength of a country's social safety net has an impact.

You'll quickly recognise some might be interrelated – you might find that age of the mother at birth and substance abuse are both linked to employment status, and so you might decide to clump them together.

Keep going until you can't think of anything else. Refer back to your 'why tree' and make sure you haven't missed anything.

Now don't worry if you haven't got lots of things on the page – five to ten is all you need. We'll call these **sectors**.

Now quickly go through them with a critical eye. You may need to separate the economy from the employment market because they might go in different directions due to technology. The economy could boom due to advances in AI and robotics, while at the same time, a lot of areas within the job market become very challenging – particularly for lower wage workers. So you might settle on employment/unemployment and the economy as two discrete sectors. There probably won't be many surprises on this list. They'll be things you'd expect to include in a typical environmental scan.

Quickly identify those you think are most significant to you achieving the answer to your strategic question. Like I said, ten is probably the maximum you want here. Hone in until you have a one or two word title for each sector, and write a brief definition if the title isn't helpful in making clear what you mean.

The next task is to briefly define a (maximum) five step scale for each of these sectors. The economy can be booming at one end of the scale and tanking at the other, with three other levels in between. The definitions don't have to be specific, but if they can be, great. It is plausible that you have identified a sector where a five step scale won't work, so don't force it.

Create a table with the names of the sectors along the top, and the scale descriptions in the rows beneath. The scales we'll call **factors**.

Stage Three: Test for Consistency

At its essential core, this tool works by choosing one **factor** from each **sector** and using these combinations to develop a 'potentially viable future'. Initially this will seem a little daunting – even with only six sectors and a maximum of five factors, you could end up with more than 4,000 combinations! However you'll quickly figure out that some combinations just don't make sense. For example, the likelihood of a scenario where employment is almost full (everyone who wants a job has one) yet substance abuse rates are astronomical, and the average age of mothers when they have their first child is below 20, is pretty low. So you might rule out this combination of factors. If any pairwise combination is 'highly unlikely', then all other combinations using that pairing can be excluded.

Use a matrix to help identify plausible sector/factor combinations[*]. Rate the pairings as 0 = manifestly inconsistent, 1 = probably inconsistent, 2 = probably consistent and 3 = highly consistent. Continue to rule out unlikely pairings until you arrive at a handful of plausible future combinations.

Stage Four: Form Scenarios

Look across the surviving combinations and choose a handful to develop into worked up scenarios. Ideally you'll do this in a way that allows you to consider at what points the scenarios diverge (either over time or due to a specific event) so that it can inform your thinking about points of influence. Use your imagination – try not to overthink it. This technique can be deceptive due to its formality and complexity. But ultimately, it provides a more objective method for arriving at a range of scenarios for how the future might unfold. And more importantly, it helps you to identify the variables that might contribute to those futures actually occurring.

Strategic Tools For Identifying Strategic Actions: TOWS Analysis

You have probably heard of a SWOT analysis. Strengths, weaknesses, opportunities and threats. And the astute reader will have observed that the acronym is changed around in the heading for this section… why?

SWOT analyses are normally conducted via a brainstorming session. Say, at the whiteboard. Which is fine. Except that different

---

[*] A worked example of this tool is available in the book resources section of my website: www.RebeccaElvy.com/BookResources

people will argue over whether something is in one section or another – for example a pessimist will describe something as a weakness, where another immediately points out "but that's an opportunity for us!".

The other reason why SWOT analyses aren't my preferred technique for strategic thinking is that they seldom arrive at concrete actions. You just end up with a pretty table with a bunch of words in each of the four quadrants, and no idea what to do with it all!

This approach is slightly different, even though the concept is the same.

On a blank piece of paper (or a whiteboard if you must!) draw up a three by three matrix. Leave the first (top left) cell blank, then head up the middle and right hand columns with "External Threats" and "External Opportunities" respectively. Then in the second row of the far left column write "Internal Weaknesses" and below that "Internal Strengths". If you are completing this exercise on your own, the 'internal' refers to you – your knowledge, your skills and so forth. The 'external' refers to everything else.

Now you can do your normal SWOT, but realise that the distinction between internal and external has been clarified – ensuring that there is less likelihood of disagreement about what should go where! Ideally you'll arrive at two to four in each of these labelled boxes[*].

Finally, in each of the four cells remaining (B2, C2, B3 and C3) you're going to create discrete actions that respond to the relevant combinations of threat and weakness, threat and strength,

[*] See www.RebeccaElvy.com/BookResources for a worked example.

opportunity and weakness and opportunity and strength. Again aim for two to three in each cell.

Now you have a list of actions you might take to influence the future. Analyse this list, as you may well find there is overlap, or things can be combined logically.

Strategic Tools For Identifying Obstacles: Force Field Analysis

The final tool we're going to look at here may well be one you come back to again and again. It's definitely one of my favourites, because it's quite visual.

At its core, Force Field Analysis is a graphical way of showing the current state, represented by one key metric (in the example I've been referring to this would be the current rates of child abuse), along with where you want to move that metric to over time (like zero). You represent that current state as a dotted line, that you will 'move' towards your target by taking actions. These actions are represented by arrows acting on the line in the desired direction. You use the size of the arrow to show how much impact each action is expected to have relative to the other actions. Then you draw arrows acting in the *opposite* direction to represent things that will prevent these actions from working. Again, the size of the obstacle arrows needs to be relative to the force of the obstacle as well. If the obstacle arrows are all large and heavy, and the action arrows are thin and light, you either need many more actions than there are obstacles, or you need to increase the efficacy of the actions to counteract the obstacles[*].

Other Tools

This is only a selection of the tools that are available – and each of them also has some variables – like a shorter version, or even a more detailed version. I've included some further examples and tools at www.RebeccaElvy.com/BookResources.

Drawing it all Together

Ultimately, strategic thinking is a way of broadening your knowledge about a topic in a disciplined way, with particular emphasis on an unknowable future. You might not need to use all of these tools to illuminate your question. But I'd encourage you to experiment anyway. Even if your topic is very narrowly focused. For example, it might be parenting related, or professionally focused in your chosen area of work.

The first time I used these tools was for a small business that my husband and I were building. We were very focused on how to grow *that particular business*. But you inevitably have to think about the economy (nationally and globally), the factors that impact on your customers, in our case the outsourcing of manufacturing to China was a factor, which also meant that the geo-political climate became a factor in our thinking. The environment (and our business's impact on it) was a factor we wanted to include, because it was important to the answers we were seeking.

---

[*] Again, there's a worked example of this tool in the Book Resources section on my website.

But. And this is a big but.

But. At some point you have to call 'enough' on the strategic analysis. The purpose of this exercise is to feed your mind with new ways of exploring your chosen topic. Not to categorically answer the question or solve the problem.

So call enough. Maybe write a short story about what you think some of the most illuminating or salient points are. Stories stick in your mind better than pages of data and analysis – so I'm suggesting this as a way to retain what you've learnt.

And then let it go.

Move on.

It's time to clarify your intent further by learning more about what already exists.

7. Research

*"If we knew what it was we were doing, it would not
be called research, would it?" Albert Einstein*

Ah, research... The procrastinator's dream... An excuse to read lots of articles and books and not actually *do* anything...

No! That's not the kind of research that I'm going to outline for you here. Instead, you need to engage in limited, targeted and purposeful research. Intentional research.

Having gained some understanding of the future circumstances and events that might relate to your 'why' – your inspiration – now is the time to figure out what's happening right now.

I want you to take a blank page and divide it into three columns. Head them up with the following headings:

- Self
- Others
- Organisations

Under each heading, quickly (without thinking too much) jot down anything you think you need to know/learn in order to accomplish your inspired purpose.

Under the topic of self, include things that relate to you: this might be about data and statistics that will inspire you or help you measure effectiveness. In the reducing child abuse example we've been using, this might be current prevalence, demographics, it should also include the things you're worried about with respect to yourself and your ability to influence this particular field, this is where Nigel can be helpful! Does Nigel think you need to be a qualified social worker or have a psychology degree? Does Nigel think you have to work within a public service agency or a school to impact this change? Does Nigel think you lack credibility in the field? Jot these down.

In the second column, jot down any questions you have about what other individuals are doing or could be doing in the area. Are there individuals already working in the field? What has been written or published about this? Books, articles? Are there online resources that might be available already? There might be a programme that a wealthy philanthropist has started (you don't need to know this yet – you uncover this fact from your research). You might know somebody already working in the field. Simply jot down every idea you can think of that relates to another individual.

Lastly, write down anything you can think of that you need to know or already know but need to investigate further about what organisations are doing in this field. Social services or child services in your jurisdiction. What not-for-profits are working in this area, church groups, charities? What research are universities currently undertaking? Is there a school with an active programme in this area?

Remember, the important thing here is to capture the question, not the answer. If you already know a partial answer to the question, that's OK too, write that down as well, but don't worry if what you end up with is a list of questions without answers.

Next, I want you to review your lists with an intensely critical eye. Deeply sceptical. Make sure you thank Nigel for his help and let him know that you've got this step! Ask yourself: "Does not knowing the answer to this question stop me from getting started right now?" Be honest. I mean really honest. Because Nigel will still be popping up in the background saying really helpful things like "nobody will take you seriously without a social work degree... you've never worked in this field". And the worst part is that he sounds very convincing, and it appeals to our desire to be seen as competent and not be embarrassed. But let me tell you a little secret. If gaining a social work degree enabled you to prevent child abuse from occurring, it would already have been prevented! Because lots of people have social work degrees. Lots of people work in the field. The entire point of finding your inspiration was to recognise the gaps you see in the world between what is and what could be. If the answer was readily available in the form of a training course or a college degree, there'd no longer be a gap!

A simple tick or cross next to each one will suffice here. Do you need to know it now, or not?

Don't worry, you're going to keep this list – you'll probably add to it. And some of the things you put a 'cross' next to now will become 'ticks' later on as you progress through your work.

Once you have identified which items have ticks next to them – the things you really need to learn or find out – look across them for any themes or commonalities. You're looking for the way to maximise the impact of your learning while minimising the time. The purpose of this exercise is to satisfy Nigel that you don't know everything, but you know what you need to know right now.

Then turn the list into actions.

In the example we're using, my tick list looked something like this:

- Read two to three academic articles on the causes of child abuse (and build a reading list of other articles from the reference sections to spread out – one per week)
- Speak to my sister, who is a foster parent and works closely with social workers and the child services support agencies, about what the issues are, what's going on, what she'd do if she could wave a magic wand
- Explore the published (web) services and information for the main child support agency in my jurisdiction, and the two to three main not-for-profit agencies offering services in this area, with a spread of assumptions about causes (e.g. One that focuses on poverty reduction, one that focuses on parenting skills, and one that focuses on helping kids escape from child abuse)
- Read the course marketing materials for one to two social work qualifications so that I know what they teach

And that's it.

This is a small number of immediately actionable steps that will increase my knowledge, placate Nigel (for now) and, not coincidentally, provide a multitude of sources of inspiration to keep me going.

But here's the key thing. It is vital that you stop when you get to the end of this list. I want you to create a new habit. You are going to pull out the original three columned page once a month – no more – and amend it (add, remove, modify) and repeat the entire exercise – ultimately arriving at three to five immediately actionable steps that you will undertake in the coming month and *no more*. When we are tackling something that feels big and scary to us, our tendency is to procrastinate by convincing ourselves that we need more information, more knowledge, more qualifications, more connections. More. More. More.

What I hope to show you through the exercise we've just completed is that while it is absolutely true that you don't know everything, it's also true that you don't *need* to know everything. And if you later discover that you *do* need to know something, learn it then!

In fact, I want to let you in on a really important secret. Sometimes *not* knowing everything – even anything – is more helpful than knowing a lot.

A colleague and inspiration of mine who lives in Denmark, drew my attention to a fabulous article about a Swedish chemist, Sven Hovmöller, who had been grappling with a particularly gnarly scientific problem for years. Eventually, he engaged his 10-year-old son in assisting him with the problem, after realising that Linus – the 10-year-old – was better at Sudoku puzzles. They cracked it in two days.

> *"Linus's main contribution was coming at it with an absolutely clear mind, being smart and able to put the puzzle together. I sort of knew too many things and when I tried to do it myself, your brain just gets exhausted by all the different things you keep in your head at the same time. With a fresh, empty brain so to speak, you can do something. When solving problems, it is always good to have someone to discuss it with."*
> *Sven Hovmöller, in New Scientist*

Sometimes you can know too much. Make sure you tell that to Nigel! Being expert can tangle you up in being right. And innovation and creativity isn't going to come from what is already known about being right – it's going to come from something completely unknown that kind of 'accidentally' turns out to be right. Nigel will encourage you to read, and research, and read, and research, and read… because while you're reading and researching, he knows you aren't doing anything dangerous. You've done both of those things many times before, and you're still here, and in fact if you think about your schooling, reading and research are often rewarded with praise and good grades!

It's what you *do* with the new knowledge that actually matters though. Think of it like a rough sketch. You're trying to build up a very general outline of what exists already. What is already known. And that is all. Remember you can always delve into the detail later if it turns out that knowing a lot about that thing is essential to your plan!

I have a habit I like to call "procrastination by research". It's a funny sort of thing because it seems like I'm busy! But really I'm delaying and deferring in the hope that I'm going to find some sort of magical insight that makes everything safe and easy.

Let me say it again. That magic bullet probably doesn't exist, and certainly hasn't been found yet!

Relatively recently I decided to stop reading academic articles about my chosen field. On the one hand, that's incredibly frustrating, because I know that some fascinating research is going on in the fields of leadership and organisational psychology. But I also know that only the most robust research makes it through to the academic journals. They tend to be incredibly risk averse when it comes to ground-breaking research. Furthermore, they tend to stick rather rigidly within their discipline. I learned a long time ago that my best ideas come from smashing two disciplines together in a rather violent way and seeing what happens. I synthesise basic knowledge from multiple disciplines, rather than going deep into one. I'm a sort of polymath I suppose.

Knowing this has given me permission to stop seeking the answers in someone else's research.

Does this mean that I run the risk of traversing territory that is already well-known and understood? Sure.

But let me tell you a little secret.

The best way to learn new knowledge isn't to read it in a journal. It's to figure it out for yourself and then confirm it by stumbling across the way someone else already proved it. You know you came up with it independently! And now you're on a par (at least in terms of your thinking) with some of the best minds in the world! So what if you didn't write the journal article first!

I know what you're saying. This is all very well, but how do I find the sweet spot between just enough research to 'roughly sketch' the landscape in the area I'm interested in, versus getting lost in the quagmire of analysis paralysis or procrastination by research?

My answer (you may well come up with your own) is to gamify it. Make a list of the topics you want to research, and set a timer for – say – five minutes. In that five minutes, your job is to find as much information as you can about that topic. Something like the Evernote clipper tool could be useful here – capture links to useful articles, names of prominent thinkers in your field, names of organisations working in the area, websites dedicated to the topic, communities of practitioners… you have five minutes to find as much as you can.

Then, set the timer again, for no more than five minutes, turn all that you've learned into a mind map. Then put it away.

Repeat for the next topic on your list.

I also suggest that if your list of topics is long (and it may be), that you force yourself to prioritise the list and you stop at 10 topics.

This gives you 100 minutes of dedicated research time. That's a fair bit!

Just remember, this is only your cursory scan. If you determine later that knowing more about a topic is vital to your work, you can return to it. Better still, you've now got a fabulous mind-map and list of resources and links to existing material to get you started!

8. Planning And Goal Setting

"Setting goals is the first step in turning the invisible into the visible." Tony Robbins

So you've developed a broad knowledge of the strategic factors that may influence the field you're working in. You've carried out some research that ensures you have more knowledge than the average person interested in the area (and better still, you know where to go to deepen or broaden that knowledge, should you need to…)

What next?

It's time to set some goals and create a plan to achieve them. It's time to take the abstract and make it concrete. It's time to get real.

Why Do I Need To Set Goals?

First, there is a body of research that scientifically supports the power of *effective* goal setting on achievement.

A small study by psychologist Dr. Gail Matthews of Michigan State University found that 76% of participants who *wrote down their goals* actually achieved them, compared with just 43% for those who just thought about their goals.

In a meta-analysis of the research on goal setting, a team of researchers at the Centre for Research Based Management[*] found that:

- Difficult and challenging goals have a moderately positive effect on performance
- Clear, specific goals have a moderately positive effect on performance
- Specific and challenging goals can have a negative effect on performance when the individual doesn't already possess the requisite skill to achieve them
- When the task is especially complex, learning goals (i.e. a goal to learn a particular skill or competency) have a positive effect on performance
- Goals need to include both short-term and long-term deliverables to be effective (as opposed to just long-term)
- Goal setting is more effective when there is also specific and timely feedback
- Creating implementation intent (if this happens, then I'll do that) to support goals makes it more likely they will be achieved
- Goals with a relationship to personal interests are more likely to be achieved than those that are unrelated

---

[*] Dr Eric Barends, Barbara Janssen and Cedric Velghe, with the support of Professor Rob Briner and Professor Denise Rousseau of Center for Evidence Based Management (CEBMa)

- People who naturally have a learning orientation (or growth mindset) are more likely to achieve their goals than those who don't

In addition, anecdotally, every 'top ten things successful people do' article I've ever read lists setting clear goals as important… so there must be something to it beyond clickbait!

The second reason is really simple. Inspiration isn't enough by itself. You can run around the world with lots of inspiration for weeks, and you may even get some things done during that time, but eventually, even with the best will in the world, inspiration will wane if it isn't being fuelled by measurable progress. To make progress that is measurable, you need to articulate what you are going to do in a way that is meaningful to you. And you need to measure it.

What you need to do is take the strategic thinking work you completed – what might or could happen, the (light) research you've done – what already is, and turn that into goals that inspire you and are directly connected to your 'why'.

What we've started to do here – or at least what we're aiming to do – is to sketch out the outline of a pathway between where we are now, and where we want to be. We are literally bridging the gap. You remember that gap we talked about at the beginning of the book? That thing that makes you uneasy or dissatisfied? You're plotting a course between what is, and what could be.

So your goal is the 'what could be'. But it's more than that. It needs to factor in what you learned from the strategic thinking exercises, it needs to take account of the research you carried out and it needs to do this while remaining true to what inspired you in the first place.

So for the example I've been using so far in this book, about reducing child abuse... my goal might be something like:

"Recognising that the vast majority of public policy and social service interventions aimed at reducing violence against children focus on treating symptoms rather than causes, and are too often the ambulance at the bottom of the cliff rather than the fence at the top of the cliff, I will develop three variations on a hypothesis about the causes of violence against children, along with one or more potential treatment options. Within five years, I will design and test these hypotheses to determine their effectiveness. In addition I will be responsive to new information that comes into the field – either from external sources or from my own experimentation, on the basis that my hypotheses can be improved with new information."

Now this is rather wordy, but it captures my 'dissatisfaction point', it factors in my research and strategic thinking (largely by recognising that progress in this area is incredibly slow), and it provides me with a set of concrete deliverables that will empower me to take *more* action at the end.

I also allow myself space to get there faster than I expected. It isn't my plan to take five years to do this, just because that was my goal. If one of my hypotheses turns out to be a roaring success, then I need to recalibrate immediately (which we'll get to in a later chapter) to accelerate progress to the ultimate goal, which is the reduction or abolition of violence against kids.

Having this goal clearly set out is really important. Let me explain why.

What's my goal? Stop child abuse. What am I doing today? Um... going to work... walking the dog... Yeah, that's probably not going to get you there. You need to go from macro, right down to micro.

To get to the goal, I now have to make actual plans. Specific actions and tasks that I accomplish on a much shorter-term basis. A set of daily habits, weekly tasks, monthly objectives... you get the point. And as scary as it might seem if your goal is big, hairy and audacious, this really matters because otherwise you will be overwhelmed.

Just a quick note from Nigel though, be wary of 'false tasks'. Tasks that seem credibly connected to your goal, but ultimately bog you down in make-busy-work... more research, more reading, more more more... things that feel like activity but actually don't get you measurably closer to your goal, and *in fact* may freak you out to the point where you actually give up... which remember is exactly what Nigel would like more than anything in the whole world!

So back to the goal – the importance of having it clearly set out...

In spite of all the hard work you've done to this point – the strategic thinking, the research, the soul-searching inspiration seeking – you aren't able to predict the future. AND once you invest in your plan, all that effort, energy, enthusiasm that you pour into those daily goals, and weekly tasks, monthly objectives, you begin to feel invested in what you've committed to.

Now investment is mostly a good thing. Feeling invested means you care, and you're driven and have strong intent – that's good. But investment can make it harder for you to innovate or stray off the beaten path if/when you realise that what you originally set out to do isn't quite working.

That sketched out path actually takes you perilously close to the edge of a dangerous ravine, and you can see at the edge of your vision, a well-trodden trail, with marker posts along the way… yet you persist along the dangerous ravine because that's what you wrote down and committed to. Having the clearly spelt out goal, and reminding yourself of it on a frequent basis, helps you remember that the destination is what's important here.

This isn't a situation where the journey is more important than the destination. In fact, what's actually important, is recognising that you don't know enough to accurately map the journey, so part of your job is to be responsive and open to the idea that an alternate route will reveal itself at the appropriate time, and that you should take it to see where it leads.

By the way, there is a substantial body of evidence building around the important principle that you find what you are looking for and regularly paying attention to. So while we talked about mindfulness earlier, hone this practice to assist you with regularly seeking alternate pathways. Be open to redrafting your plan. Don't be precious about it. Treat it like you would a map. It includes multiple true paths, and one intended route. But if something happens and that intended route is not viable, or there is clearly a shorter and more effective route just over there that wasn't apparent on the map, grasp it with both hands! Remember the destination and why you want to get there! It'll be worth it, I promise.

So that's all very well, but how do you do this? A metaphorical map is a lovely idea, but all I have is a mostly blank sheet of paper with a far distant goal written on it! That's a great question. And in fact, good questions are exactly what you need now. So settle in for a deeply interrogative session…

With your goal at the top centre of a blank page (I suggest landscape rather than portrait), start by asking: "what would have to be true for this to occur?" and jot down whatever springs to mind. In the example I'm using, for my goal to occur, I would need to have the results of testing multiple hypotheses.

"What would need to be true for this to occur?" I would need to design, and then test, these hypotheses.

"What would need to be true for this to occur?" I would need a credible theory as to why child abuse occurs.

"What would need to be true for this to occur?" I would need to interview social workers to understand their perspectives.

"What would need to be true for this to occur?"…

You get the picture. This is a little like the Why-Tree from the strategic thinking chapter, but with a slightly different emphasis.

Now it's important to note that there can – and should – be more than one answer to these questions, and that each answer creates its own branch of logic that you need to chase down and clarify. That's great. Instead of being where you are now and feeling like you need to figure out the *right* next step to get things started, you actually have multiple actions that will get you on your path. You don't have to do all of them, but you can probably do more than one. Some of these paths will prove fruitless, so I suggest you don't put all your eggs in one basket.

The next step, with your very 'tree-like' goal analysis, is to go through each of the answers and allocate an indicative time to that thing. How long would it take to interview social workers, for example. And jot that down. Maybe use a different coloured pen. What you're starting to identify is a critical path from where you are, to where you want to be. Or, perhaps more importantly, several critical paths!

Feel free to annotate these tasks in other ways. It's highly likely that some of the tasks will be very similar, and could potentially be combined. Some of the tasks will be pre-requisites to tasks in other branches, and therefore you know they have to happen first, so there's a great deal of value in pursuing both those paths simultaneously, because it will be efficient use of your effort. The last task here is to plot these tasks out into a timeframe. You can populate a calendar, if you're familiar with project management methods, you might choose a Gantt chart for this purpose.

You now have a path – or several paths – to help you achieve this goal! But my suspicion is, if you're anything like me and you've chosen a goal that would make normal folks quiver with dread and fear, there's probably still some more work to be done before you really feel like you know what you need to do.

Highlight the tasks that you've identified that happen in roughly the first six months to one year. Reword these tasks so that they become goals in their own right, and importantly, this is the time to get SMART[*]. I actually prefer SMARTER. Because you're going to have to be "smarter than the average bear" to achieve the things you've got in mind!

Here's my thoughts on SMARTER Goals:

Specific

Generally, the S in SMART is specific. A goal must be specific, not general. Not "exercise more", but "go for a 20 minute run every other day". Exercise more could mean that you go to the gym once a month, instead of not at all – which could mean a significant improvement in overall health and wellbeing, but it could also mean going to the gym 28 times instead of 27. Or doing one jumping-jack a year... or touching your toes on Tuesdays... who knows!

Measurable/Meaningful

Generally this model appears with measurable in the 'M' slot, which largely comes from asking yourself 'how would I know if this had been achieved'? It generally means some sort of metric will appear in the description of the goal. A solid 'specific' goal is going

---

[*] It is generally accepted that the concept of SMART goals first appeared in 1981 in a paper called "There's a SMART Way to Write Management's Goals and Objectives" by George T. Doran

to lean towards being measurable anyway, because it's pretty hard to be specific without quantifying the goal in some way. In the example we used above, 'a 20 minute run every other day', we have two measurable things: the length of the run, and the frequency of the run. In this case, both types of measurement are important, because without the duration of the run, you could just jog to the kitchen sink and back, and without the frequency, you could simply go for a single 20 minute run and you would have met your goal. Unless going for a run one time is your goal, this probably isn't sufficient.

The meaningful version is a useful addition too. If you don't care about the goal – if it isn't connected to your 'why' – you probably aren't going to follow through with it. Certainly not when it gets tricky or unclear what you need to do next. So do a double-check and make sure the goal is meaningful to you – otherwise it can be the SMARTest goal in the world, but you still won't get there.

Attainable/Achievable/Accountable/Agreed/Ambitious

The 'a' in SMART has proven to be fairly useful, and varies more than any other letter in the acronym.

Attainable and achievable are more or less the same thing. But we need a brief chat here about comfort zones.

Michael Hyatt, in his book *Your Best Year Ever*, uses a model for thinking about goals in terms of three levels of comfort. He says too many people set goals that are well inside their comfort zone. These goals are a walk in the park, and don't really require any particular strain or effort to achieve them. Organisations in particular are very bad at doing this – only setting goals that management know will be achieved. That's not what is intended by attainable or achievable. As Hyatt points out, goals that are inside your comfort zone don't energise you. In fact it can be so hard to get motivated that you use more energy to do them than you would to do something a bit more **ambitious**.

But he also advises against setting goals in the 'delusional zone'. Hyatt refers to this as the area where the goal is super-exciting to begin with but ultimately becomes demotivating as reality sinks in, and the magnitude of the challenge becomes apparent.

Instead, the aim is to create goals that are in the **discomfort** zone. Or the Goldilocks zone. Or the development zone. Something that will take some effort. Something that requires you to become something you aren't right now. That you'll need to develop new skills for, or do something you've never done before, or something that scares you just the right amount, or that you'll need help with.

Accountable and agreed are, again, kind of the same thing. There's a body of evidence to suggest that it isn't enough for *just you* to know what your goals are, because you can convince yourself that what you *really* meant was actually this or actually that. No, instead you need to write them down, and tell someone about them. Ideally you tell someone who is supportive of your ambition, and possibly even invested in helping you achieve the objectives you've set. You want someone that you'll listen to when they say "hey – hang on a minute, weren't you going to do…20 minutes a day?"

Interestingly though, it's been my experience that shouting your goals from the rooftops and broadcasting them in a majorly public way can be counter-productive. You can ultimately end up feeling so hemmed in by the public accountability you've created, that you aren't able to re-evaluate the goal when new information comes along. This can mean continuing to pursue an objective, even when it's clear that it isn't going to help you accomplish your ultimate aim – and what's the point in that?

There's also a psychological effect that telling everyone you're working towards a particular goal means you repeat it so frequently that you brain begins to believe you've already done it... the counter-productive benefit of affirmations! It's pretty hard to get motivated to do something your brain thinks is already done!

Relevant/Related/Realistic

Relevant and related are also basically the same thing. If the goal you've set isn't a comprehensible step on the journey from where you are, to where you need to be, then it's going to be challenging to maintain your focus and momentum when the going gets tough. But the good thing is, it's *you* who gets to tell the story, so provided the logic makes sense to you, that's all that matters.

Goals aren't always achieved in a linear way – sometimes you need to head way over sideways to approach things from a slightly different angle.

Hopefully relevant/related is a no-brainer.

Realistic, on the other hand, is slightly trickier. Realistic is intended to protect you from overreaching. You don't want to set goals that, no matter what you do, you have no hope of achieving. That's incredibly demoralising, and not at all helpful to you achieving your ultimate objective.

You need to find that sweet spot where something is outside your comfort zone, but not in your delusional zone. Call it 'discomfort', call it 'development', call it whatever works for you, but you need to be able to define it for yourself. This is your goal. Nobody else gets to decide for you.

In fact, this is a really important point that warrants some elaboration at this juncture.

People will tell you you're tilting at windmills – that you're deluded, a dreamer, unrealistic. In fact, if your ultimate objectives are really important – like earth-shatteringly significant – some people will even be frightened... you'll be threatening their perceptions of reality and 'how the world works'.

You know how we've talked about Nigel? *Everyone has a Nigel.* He might have a different name, but everyone has one, and as soon as you start doing things that might create change for others, you can expect these other Nigels to pipe up and say something...

From your perspective, this manifests as resistance to your ideas... even downright undermining or criticism.

I'm not going to tell you to ignore this – because you're human, and your version of Nigel likes to be liked. But you'll need to find a way to make peace with it. To shut it out and persist anyway. The worst thing is, sometimes those very people who are resisting what you are doing are those closest to you. In those cases, they aren't necessarily resisting what you are trying to create or change *per se.* More likely, they are resisting the changes that will manifest in *you* as you become the sort of person capable of achieving that kind of objective.

This is particularly the case for parents (who always seem to have a set of pre-conceived ideas about what their children will or won't accomplish), partners/spouses (who can feel very unsettled or threatened when one party seems to be developing themselves more quickly, and they feel like you might be leaving them behind) and friends who might be used to seeing themselves as more accomplished and successful than you. Everyone's ego makes sense of the world in its own way – and threatening these perceptions can create quite significant adverse reactions. You'll need to work out whether and how to address these reactions – ranging from leaving the relationship through to enlisting that person's support for your objective.

All of this is simply a way of letting you know that people close to you aren't always the best judge of how realistic a particular goal is. You know in your gut whether you think it is doable or not. I don't mean whether it is comfortable or not, but whether – with a lot of hard work and determination – it could be achieved. And at the end of the day, your view is the only one that actually matters. Because you are the one that has to be inspired by it. You are the one who has to leap out of bed in the morning to get it done – often on top of a bunch of other normal 'day-job' activities. You are the one who has to find the brute strength and will-power to keep going when the approach you were taking turns out to be unsuccessful. This is where a little bit of optimism can be very helpful.

Timebound/Timed

Now I don't know about you, but if you're anything like me, a good deadline is important. Of course, they never feel like 'good' deadlines at the point they're bearing down upon you, but without a date, a deadline, why would you ever get it done? It can always be more finished, more perfect, more tidy, more well-developed, more consulted, more 'insert-favourite-adjective-here'.

You need to put a timeline on it, or it will drag on forever. And ever. So set a date. Build that date into the description of your goal. Mark it on your calendar. Commit it to memory. It's important, because you need to work back from it to set the sub-tasks within the goal.

Here's the important point though. When *you* set yourself a deadline, *you* can easily move it. Do you see the problem here?

There are good reasons and bad reasons to change the deadline. They basically fit into two categories: Nigel-related reasons and all other reasons. Your job is to be able to tell the difference.

Nigel will tell you it isn't ready yet. It needs more work. The timing isn't quite right because x, y and z are happening at or around the same time… These aren't real reasons. They're actually excuses. But Nigel disguises them as reasons so that you might not notice it's coming from him.

The other type of reasons are *actual* reasons. Like when you work back with the sub-tasks to create the detail underneath the goal, and you realise that it literally isn't possible to do all the things necessary to achieve the goal.

Sometimes though, Nigel disguises his fear-based excuses as *exactly* this kind of reason! So you need to interrogate the reason pretty thoroughly before deciding whether to accept it or not.

Ask some good questions:

- What would happen if I proceeded anyway?
- Could I accomplish the goal in a different way that removed the need for that stage?
- Is there a better way?
- Is this mission critical?

I'm sure you can think of some more, but in essence you are 'stress-testing' the reason. Before you change the deadline you need to be absolutely sure that the reason is 'real'.

Why? Because if you know it's not real (and believe me, if it's a Nigel-related reason, *he* knows even if you don't!) then you have commenced a descent down a very slippery slope indeed. If you know that you've moved the deadline once for a 'made-up' reason, you can easily do it again. Why not? It clearly isn't a real deadline – you made it up in the first place, didn't you?

If you break this pact with yourself for anything other than a *bona fide* reason, you'll know it isn't real, and you won't take it seriously. It won't have the effect it's supposed to have, which is driving you to get more done, keeping the pressure on, and keeping you motivated when the going gets tough.

Make a commitment to yourself when you set the deadline. By all means do some work first to ensure it's realistic, but ultimately, you are making a promise to yourself, and you need to keep it.

It is ultimately better to not quite meet your deadline, but continue to strive for it up until the moment it's clear you cannot make it, than to move it at the drop of a hat.

Why?

Two reasons:

- You'll show Nigel you're serious, and it will build your confidence and trust in yourself
- Some of the greatest creativity emerges from the most rigid constraints. Ask any brilliant architect whether they'd rather have a flat, vacant lot with no planning constraints or a steep rocky slope with protected trees to work with... Working within difficult constraints forces creative solutions.

Energising/Exciting/Emotional/Ethical

Energising, exciting and emotional should be a no-brainer, but I'll say it anyway.

If you ain't feeling it, you ain't gonna get it done.

It takes a lot of extra oomph to do something that is hard. Particularly given there is no beaten path, no roadmap. You're doing this thing because nobody else has succeeded, right? You need to *feel* it. You need to believe it's important. You need to be passionate and empowered by the energy you get from just thinking about what will happen if you succeed.

This needs to be more than just "ooh, I had a good sleep last night, I'm feeling good" kind of energy – it needs to make you go into a state of 'flow' and not notice that time is passing. It needs to bring you joy. It needs to fill you up, even when you are physically tired. If you are worried you don't quite have this, you may need to go back and revisit your inspiration. Have you really found it?

The ethical piece is a little different, and to be honest, I think it's really important. It's also challenging, because ethics and morality are, believe it or not, subjective. The Nazis believed they were doing the right thing, or at least many of them did.

Now I'm not going to turn this into a lesson on morality. But I'm just going to say that I'm not writing this book so that people can commit more successful atrocities. Yet I'm aware that if I make no mention of morality or ethics, then I could in fact be doing exactly that.

So instead of trying to set out a moral code, I'm just going to say this: You need to ensure that love is what is driving you, not ego, and not fear.

Leadership is amoral. Strictly speaking, it doesn't distinguish between right and wrong. Good and bad. The morality of leadership is determined by the goal and the morality of the leader. That's why I put ethics here in this section.

It's also why, later on in the book, you'll find a section on unintended consequences. Because sometimes your intent is just and good, but the knock-on impacts of what you are doing have serious negative consequences for a group of people (or things) that you hadn't considered at the outset. Economists tend to refer to these as externalities, or perverse incentives. Ultimately it doesn't matter what you call them, you didn't mean it to happen, but it did. You've got to own the impact of that, and redress the consequences as best you can.

Be driven by love. Not ego or fear. And do no harm.

Recorded/Reviewed

I'm sorry about this, but you gotta write it all down. With quite a bit of detail.

This is your personal accountability. It's all very well to tell someone else the high-level outline of the plan, but (unless you have a coach) it's unlikely that you're going to tell them about the 73,000 fliers you plan to deliver in phase three, or the website you'll create to blog about your progress, or the research you'll need to do into carbon harvesting facilities in China.

You've probably made a bunch of notes to this point, but now that you have the complete picture, you should be able to capture the key points into a fairly meaty goal description, preceded by a good amount of the contextual strategic thinking and research you completed.

You should clearly spell out your hypothesis. You need to be able to refer to, and test, this hypothesis on a fairly regular basis while you are implementing your plan. And you need to describe how you'd know if you were successful – begin with the end in mind, as they say. I've included a template for recording SMARTER goals in the book resources page on my website[*].

And once you've written it all down, it's really important that you review it frequently. I don't mean once it's finished, and you come back and evaluate what worked and what didn't, I mean you print it out and put it somewhere you can see it, and ideally, you read it daily – at least lightly, to remind yourself of what you are aiming for.

---

[*] www.RebeccaElvy.com/BookResources

In his Best Year Ever system, Michael Hyatt recommends you review your goals every day and ask yourself the question "what is the one thing I will do today to move closer to achieving this goal.

The point of this is recency. And momentum. You want your goal to be top-of-mind when you are moving through your day. Why?

Because you need to be on the lookout for opportunities. The act of reviewing the goal every day, and reminding yourself of it with a degree of detail, means it is right there, and your brain is asking questions about how to do it. Of course you don't have all the answers – you can't possibly have all the answers, or even all the next steps – remember this is a really big audacious goal you've set – not just a run-of-the-mill New Year's Resolution! You want (and need) your brain to be working on it even when you aren't. You want your brain to hear that article on the television news and file it away as potentially useful for achieving your goal. You want your brain to spot the new release book at the bookstore written by someone who has done this kind of thing before, and think… "oooh, that could be useful". You want your brain to overhear that conversation on the bus or train that gives you another piece in the jigsaw puzzle. Not the complete picture yet, but collecting the pieces, one by one.

Have you ever noticed that some of the biggest problems you've ever solved come to you in what feels like a 'stroke of genius' when you aren't even thinking about the problem directly? Like in the shower. Or after a good night's rest. Or after exercise. Your brain, with the right input, will work away on the problem in the background while you go about your daily life. It's pretty neat like that.

Now this doesn't mean that you can just read your goal every day and trust that it will solve itself. It might, but hope is not a strategy! You do have to actively engage with the problem – which is why you should review your goal, while asking yourself "what is the one thing I will do today to move this forward?" You might also notice that I use the word "will" in that statement. Not could, not can, not might, but **will**.

This is important too. You need to clearly state your intent as an action. "I will do this" is a much more powerful action-oriented statement than "I could do this" or "I might do that". Use language to your advantage. Don't slip into passive or inactive language, because it is a slippery slope from there to inertia... which you'll learn more about in our next section.

Concluding Thoughts About Intent

Of all the four phases covered in this book – inspiration, intent, impact and insight – this is by far Nigel's favourite. It's full of the most compelling possibilities for him to persuade you to give up and have a latte.

Unlike inspiration which, while daunting, is clearly exciting and purposeful and 'safe', this phase is filled with specific things that Nigel can freak you out about.

Dates, tasks, deliverables – these are the stuff that fears are made of.

Furthermore, the strategic thinking phase is rich for imaginary anxieties about what might go wrong, the research phase is filled with reasons (legitimate sounding ones) for why more research (also known as procrastination) would be better than getting started, and the planning and goal-setting phase is just plain daunting.

Don't let him get you down. You got this.

Part Four: Overcoming Inertia 🦋

9. The Power Of Momentum

Excellent. Now you are inspired. You have overcome indecision. And you have clearly and specifically set your intent. It's time to get moving… to overcome inertia.

Have you ever push-started a car?

It's less of a thing these days, as modern cars tend to be more reliable (or maybe we simply don't keep them for as long) but it used to be that cars would breakdown – particularly their batteries would run down if you accidentally left the lights on. And to get them started again, you either needed another car with jumper cables so that you could use *its* battery to start your car *or* you needed someone to give you a push so you could 'bumpstart' the car once it was moving.

I was on the pushing end of this a few times as a kid. (I also did it once in high-heels on the grounds of the Australian Federal Parliament, but that's another story!) And the hardest thing was getting the vehicle moving from stationary. Once it was moving a little bit, it became easier and easier to speed it up further, and to keep it moving. Why? Because the vehicle's own weight started to gain momentum of its own. It was moving, so it would keep moving with only enough force exerted to overcome the friction from the air and a little bit of friction and resistance from the tires and axle.

Changing habits and altering the course of your otherwise relatively comfortable life is like that too.

Compound that effect if you are also talking about a goal that impacts on other people, and even more if your goal involves changing entire systems (like public policy, social service delivery or a commercial entity). All of those people and systems have their own momentum, that gently but forcefully carries them on in the direction they are already going.

Early in my public service career, a senior leader I worked for likened changing big systems to altering the course of a large ship. Or even a fleet. It is very hard to change direction once it has built up a head of steam, and when there is more than one entity involved, the change in direction must be incredibly tightly orchestrated and co-ordinated if it is going to have the desired effect quickly and efficiently.

Now Nigel likes this fact. He likes it for a couple of reasons.

First, it means that there isn't always any discernible impact from your efforts for a while once you start.

"See!" he says, "it's not working, I told you so!"

Second, he can play on your fears even more than at any other stage to this point...

"It's going to be really hard to move this beast around, what if you pour all your efforts and hard work into getting the fleet to start changing course only to realise you've sent it in the wrong direction? Getting it to turn back again will be even more difficult!"

Nigel would really like you to give up and go back to your safe, routine life. He doesn't really like the idea of directing fleets of ships... especially through potentially turbulent seas.

At this point, I need to remind you that the ocean-going vessel story is **just a metaphor**. Unless your goal is *actually* to redirect a flotilla, it's just a collection of words that create some mental imagery for you. And as with all metaphors, you should only use them when they are useful to you.

In this case, when you feel a little discouraged that you aren't seeing the magnitude of results that you'd hoped as quickly as you'd hoped, then remember that it is tricky to start something moving, and even harder to change its direction (but there are ways that you can divert it without directly resisting the forces at play).

Think about nudges.

Sometimes, when an object – a heavy object – is moving at pace in a particular direction, a gentle nudge on the *side* can help it change direction quite quickly. This works best when it is only a minor correction that is needed. It's less effective if you actually need the object to go in the opposite direction than the one it was headed in.

When you *do* need to do a complete 180 degree direction shift, you need to seriously consider whether it will be more effective to exert directly opposite (and greater) pressure to get the object to stop completely, then reverse OR to use a sequence of gentle side-nudges to carefully steer the object round in a complete 180 degrees without directly opposing its momentum.

Sorry for the physics lesson, but sometimes the mental imagery is useful – the trick is figuring out how to apply it to non-physical objects!

But to extend the metaphor just a little, you've now got yourself in motion… how do you maintain that when the world conspires to resist your efforts?

10. Remaining Inspired

*"Only those who risk going too far can possibly find
out how far one can go." T. S. Eliot*

Have you ever run a marathon?

I haven't, and to be honest it holds no appeal for me – so I'm not a good case study for this example! I do understand though, that people who do it find it beneficial. Students in the third year of their psychology degree at Bangor University, for example, are encouraged to run a marathon during their final semester, as part of the module on positive and motivational psychology. The timing of the marathon run is no accident. The end of university study can be a daunting and scary time… but if you've run a marathon as *well* as completed your studies, I suspect you feel a little bit bulletproof!

But if you've ever spent time observing marathon runners during the event, you'll notice that – in the absence of a genuine medical emergency – the time when most runners pull out of the race is during what's known as the 'messy middle'. Not the first 10 miles when the actual distance left to run is at its most daunting, and not the last six miles, when the physical exhaustion is at its absolute peak, but the 10 or so miles in between when the end is not in sight, and the psychological game is the decider. Those runners who are able to keep going when they are physically hurting but still too far from the finish to dig deep and push are playing a different mental game… It's not that they are in better physical condition (it happens relatively equally throughout the field, including those who were on track to make a good time, and those who are running for the personal satisfaction of ticking 'complete a marathon' off their bucket list). The difference is their mental condition.

Andy Barton, writing for The Guardian[*] talks about 12 steps to running a marathon:

- Getting your language right
- Visualising the right things
- Practising the bad bits in your head (and the good bits too)
- Renaming your emotions (e.g. anxiety becomes excitement)
- Find your routine
- Set small goals
- Focus on the process not just the outcome
- Find a way to block bad thoughts
- Look up and around (not just at the road)
- Smile
- Think of the race as a staging post, not an outcome (in case you can't finish)
- Remember how far you've come

Largely, it boils down to staying connected with their 'why'. Why are they running this marathon? What happens if they complete it? What happens if they don't? Do they have pledges for charity that

[*] "How to run a marathon in your mind: 12 tips for winning the mental fight" accessed at https://www.theguardian.com/lifeandstyle/the-running-blog/2015/apr/16/how-to-run-a-marathon-12-tips-mental-fight

won't be completed if they don't finish? Do they have public accountability and not want to let anybody down? Are they running as part of a team?

All of these things tend to help runners get through the messy middle. It's about mental toughness and clarity about the inspiration that got them registered for the race in the first place.

So what does this have to do with you and your big audacious goal? (Assuming your goal isn't to run a marathon!)

Turns out, quite a lot.

It's hard to figure out exactly where the messy middle is going to be for your goal. It could be the day after you begin. It could be a couple of weeks in. It could be months in. But it's likely to be at a point when you've invested a lot of energy and effort, you're feeling exhausted by the effort, and you can't tell yet whether you're having any impact at all...

Cue... Nigel.

"Are you sure it's worth it? It doesn't seem to be working. Maybe it just isn't possible, after all..."

You can bet he's got something to say for pretty much every scenario you can think of! But remember, his primary purpose is to **prevent** you from making changes. He finds them life-threateningly scary. He can't hear your rational brain pointing out all the reasons why he's wrong. He can only sense your overwhelm and pounce on it...

Now it's probably unrealistic to think that you can avoid overwhelm completely. This is a big goal, right! Otherwise you would have done it already, and there'd be no need for books like this one!

What you need to do, enlisting the help and support of your rational brain when you *aren't* physically and emotionally exhausted, is to anticipate this phase, and deliberately design a bunch of things into your process that will greatly enhance your likelihood of overcoming the messy middle. Nothing can guarantee success – but you can improve the odds.

Mindfulness

You've probably figured out by now that I'm an avid proponent of a reasonably well developed mindfulness practice as a healthy foundation for living a life less ordinary. The same thing applies here. Mindfulness (usually built from some form of deliberate meditation practice) enables you to stand apart from your thoughts and observe them, rather than participating in them. This makes it harder for Nigel to get airtime, and easier for your logical brain to actually evaluate the reality of the situation.

In addition, realising that there is 'only now' can be incredibly liberating. What do I mean by that? You only have this moment. And this one. And this one. And they are all present moments. Once you've had them, you have a memory of them (which you might think of as the past) and before you have them, you have some *anticipation* of them (which you might think of as planning or in some cases, anxiety and worry). But those aren't real. They are memories, and worries. They don't *actually* exist. Only this present moment exists. Right here. Right now.

Focusing on this moment right now, and cutting it off from your memories of the past and your anticipation of the future is a way to break the uber-goal into much smaller and more manageable pieces. You only have to focus on what to do right NOW. Not what to do next, or after that, or next week.

This might seem counter-intuitive, given how much of this book has been dedicated to the art of setting goals and creating plans. But remember that I haven't asked you to create an exhaustive list of all the things you have to do. You have a clear goal, and an understanding of the context in which you are operating, but not a step by step instruction guide. That simply isn't practical, helpful or even possible. So the work you've done on strategic thinking (context and potential future context), research, and goal setting all remains. You know it's there. You get to not worry too much about it. Relax in the knowledge that it exists and that is all.

So focus on the next few minutes. Or even just this minute.

And rather than creating giant to-do lists (which will overwhelm you – Nigel will ensure that they do) just focus on what you will do today to move closer to your goal. And do that.

Visualisation

Sticking now with a technique that found mainstream acceptance via high-performance sport, I want to talk about visualisation.

Now again, some of you will be thinking I've gone all airy-fairy… but this is your big goal remember! It better be worth doing! So what's wrong with trying a few techniques that might increase your likelihood of succeeding?

I thought so.

Now don't overthink this. You've already done this – remember that 10 year vision narrative you wrote earlier? That's a really good starting place. Keep it with you, and read it whenever you feel overwhelmed or frustrated. Read it a couple of times if necessary.

If you want to get a bit more adventurous (and let's face it, you're that kind of person!) then you can 'freestyle' a visualisation exercise at any point, irrespective of whether you have your 10 year vision story with you.

Find a quiet spot and, if you can, close your eyes.

Imagine yourself in the future. Pick a time-frame that works with your goal – if you anticipate it will take five years to deliver, then it needs to be five years plus one... or if it's a one year goal, then one plus one...

Now imagine the world has changed in exactly and precisely the way you intended it to. The problem you sought to solve has been solved. In my case, violence against children has basically gone in the developed world.

Imagine that world in some detail. What is it like? What is happening that's different? What is happening to sustain the changes? How do you feel about the changes? What are you still contributing to continue the work? Are you being publicly (or privately recognised) in some way? What are the knock-on impacts of the changes? 'Meet' someone who has benefited from the change. Speak to him or her about what the changes have meant. Find out how life is different. Maybe you spend some time with several people who have benefited from your effort. Maybe they tell you what it has meant to them. Maybe they share a 'before and after' story. Maybe you visit a place you couldn't have before. Maybe you have more money or time now.

Add detail… colour, and texture, and light, and sound, and taste, and smell. Really *feel* it. The more memorable it is, the better.

Just go where it takes you, but seek out the positive feelings. You want to really bask in the good outcomes you've created. The positive changes. The benefits to others, and to yourself. These should be aligned with what motivates you… and funnily enough, you're in charge, so a good visualisation – if you get in the flow of it – will often *reveal* what motivates you, if you didn't already know!

Enjoy it. Breathe it in. Bask in the reflected glory of your accomplishments.

Remember that.

It needs to sustain you when you meet the messy middle.

Create a Vision Board

A vision board can be an excellent way to keep your goal front and centre – and it's a fantastic outlet for a little creativity along the way. Don't worry if this sounds a little bit 'la la' – there's lots of great ideas online (but don't get stuck researching!)

You're looking for a way to visually represent why you are going to tackle this crazy thing… so that every single day when you look at it, you are reminded of why you got into this insane gig in the first place.

In my case – with a goal to end violence against children, I might focus on the desired future state, using photographs and words and targets. Or if I'm feeling like a negative push might be more motivating, I could use words, triggers – and yes even pictures – of what happens if I do nothing. Unfortunately, I'm not going to find it hard to locate these images… they're on news websites and in newspapers nearly every day.

Now a vision board can be formal or informal, and it should change over time.

What do I mean by formal? I have one at the moment focused on all my goals (not just the one I'm talking about here), and I used images I found online that inspired me (think rewards and incentives) and then using a free online graphic design app, I overlaid the text and words that related to my goals and targets and habits for the year. These were all in the format of regular photographs (6" x 4") and I took the files into a photographic shop and had them printed, just like you might for your favourite holiday snaps. Then I laid them out on a cork-board with a white background. They look slick and make me happy (and inspired) every time I look at them.

Previously I have used the informal method – this is where you find a bunch of words, images, photos, things/objects that inspire you, and you can create a kind of 'collage' on a cork-board or similar. Simply lay everything out in a way that pleases you. Overlap things, put things that need to be close to each other close to each other. Tell a story. Most importantly, remember the only person who needs to understand it (and like it) is you!

The final step, once you've created your vision board, is to put it somewhere you'll see it regularly. Mine's on the wall in my office.

It is part of my morning routine to stop and look at it in some detail every day, so that my goals are never far from my mind.

This book is there… it reminds me I need to write 1,000 to 1,500 words every day. It reminds me why I'm writing the book, and most importantly, it reminds me what I want my life to be like… without losing sight of the fact that the only moment is *this* moment, and I don't want to wish my life away for something that I might accomplish in the future. So it includes things I want to enjoy and experience every day – like bedtime stories with my four year old son.

Goals in a Prominent Place

If none of these ideas appeal – or even if they do, but you want to be doubly sure you won't lose sight of what you're aiming for – you can also print out your goals and stick them somewhere prominent. Beside the bathroom mirror, tucked inside your journal or planner, inside your wallet, on a 'wallpaper' or 'lock screen' on your mobile phone, or as a screensaver on your computer. Just remember, it needs to be somewhere you'll see it often, and be reminded in some detail, of what you're aiming to achieve.

11. Laziness

"Know the true value of time; snatch, seize, and enjoy every moment of it. No idleness, no laziness, no procrastination: never put off till tomorrow what you can do today." Philip Stanhope, 4th Earl of Chesterfield

Ah laziness… how you tempt me… How Nigel adores you… Safe. Warm. Comfortable. Easy. Did I say safe?

So let's get right to the point here. One of the greatest enemies of progress is laziness.

Not lack of activity *per se*, but laziness. A preference not to do anything that is even a little bit hard. A little bit out of the ordinary. Involves even a little bit of effort.

We've talked about it before, but it warrants another mention, because laziness – and the human propensity for it – is likely to be the most plausible, not to mention inviting, reason why you won't achieve what you set out to do.

Your evolutionary journey involved significant periods of time where, like koalas, all of your energy needed to be spent on staying safe and finding food, with a little bit of reproduction and child rearing thrown in for good measure.

Did you know that koalas spend 22 hours a day sleeping because eucalyptus leaves are so low in nutritional content? Of the remaining hours in the day, the rest are spent finding and eating eucalyptus leaves… oh, with a little reproduction for – you know – survival of the species. Koalas also have horrific rates of chlamydia – but that's a topic for an entirely different book!

Not so far back in our history, we weren't that different (OK, maybe not the chlamydia part). We had to conserve all of our spare energy for either getting away from predators or finding food. All of it.

The rise of agriculture – which led to increasingly refined foods and starches that were high in calories and didn't run away – led to increasing leisure time… and we begin to see the rise of art, and culture, and more complex societies emerging. Language, communication, power, trade, commerce, warfare… All of these things begin to emerge only *after* the human diet develops enough 'redundancy' that it was safe to do so.

This is also the point at which the human brain starts to increase in size and complexity… until the brain is using a staggering 20% of all the energy consumed by the body.

So when I say you are lazy, I don't mean it as an insult. So am I. So is everybody. It's how we're wired. How we're made. But if you don't work at it, it is your default position. If you don't pay attention (and don't forget how useful Nigel is at just surreptitiously convincing you that the best thing you could possibly do is absolutely nothing!) this is exactly what you'll end up doing. Nothing.

Absolutely nothing.

Not a thing.

So how can you combat this? Are you doomed to failure before you even begin?

No. There are two things you need to do.

Habits

The first, you need to install great habits that override this tendency. Because one of the things you'll probably notice is that when something is a habit, you tend to do it on autopilot. Without thinking.

You need to ensure that your habits are progressive rather than stagnant though. What does this mean? Compare these two habits:

- Run for 30 minutes, five times a week
- Run for 30 minutes, five times a week, increasing the distance by half a mile every month, and adding five minutes every other month.

Now it's true that both are worthy goals, and there are plenty of people in the world who would be very well-served by installing the first habit. Demand for chronic health care services would no doubt plummet, particularly in the developed world... But the first habit allows a lot of latitude for variation. Or at the very least, absolute stability. I can comfortably run two and a half miles in 30 minutes, so I'll do that five times a week. Great!

Except it just moves you on to another plateau. If your goal is only to ever run two and a half miles, that might be fine – but if your goal is to run a marathon, this habit isn't going to get you there.

Now true, the second habit will take you a fair while to get to marathon running level as well, but at least it gets progressively harder every month. You aren't going to plateau. You'll keep increasing the difficulty, and eventually you'll arrive at your objective.

So your habits – the new 'programmes' you install in your brain to help make getting to your ambitious crazy scary goal a little more manageable – need to do more than just lift you to a slightly higher ledge. They need to push you to do better and more and faster on a regular basis, in a way that your brain still believes they are habits, rather than *new* activities.

The gradual increase in difficulty can't be so great that it causes you to stop, or your brain doesn't believe that it's the same habit. Otherwise Nigel gets to have his say about this exhausting new activity you've undertaken!

Mindset

You have probably heard of 'mindset' in some pretty fluffy places before… maybe on infomercials, in self-help books, and in The Secret… the idea that you just need to believe that you have abundance coming to you and focus on that abundance and you will magically have, well, abundance.

Now I want to pay no disservice to people who subscribe to this line of thinking. If it works for them, then all power to them!

Personally though, I prefer a little bit of science with my faith. So I'm going to talk here about growth mindset, rather than abundance. This is research-based, and backed by the data.

In a nutshell, a growth mindset is basically made up of two closely related things.

Self-talk that says just because you can't do something right now, doesn't mean you couldn't learn to do it if you applied yourself. This is as opposed to a fixed mindset – the belief that if you aren't born with an innate talent in a particular domain, then tough – don't bother. You aren't any good at… (insert desired skill or trait here) so forget about it.

The second component of a growth mindset is that you are in control of you. Not some external forces. Sure, things happen around you that you can't control, but you can control your reactions and responses to these things. You can change how you think about them, what you learn from them, how long you think about them.

This is not to deny that there is bad stuff out there. People lose loved ones in tragic circumstances. People are permanently disabled in accidents that weren't of their making. Relationships break up. Redundancies and lay-offs occur. Fortunes are made and lost… These things are all very serious, and can impact you in any number of ways. But **you** are in control of how you react to these events. How quickly you recover. And what you choose to do next. And after that. And the day after that.

When you put these two things together, you get a pretty powerful combination. You get a fantastically powerful tool – your brain – that you realise is under your control. That you can utilise any way that you see fit. To learn a new language, to master the art of poaching an egg, or to rid the world of famine and disease.

If you can do one of these things, what's to stop you doing the others?

Nigel, mostly. But hopefully you're getting him under control by now!

And when you have Mindset and Progressive Habits in tandem, nothing can stop you. Because your mindset will help you install new habits. Your mindset will help you recognise when an existing habit is no longer serving you well. Your mindset will help you get rid of an underperforming habit and upgrade it to a better, more awesome one. And your mindset will give you the courage and audacity to pick up a book like this one and decide that you can change the world.

And with your mindset... you will.

But Life Gets In The Way...

Before we move on, though, I don't want to just leave you hanging there. Because you're hopefully convinced that you can change your mindset and create some powerful and empowering habits... but there's a bit of bumpy ground between here and there.

So here are a few tips that will help you get started.

The first is the 5 Second Rule, and you can find it in a fabulous book called (surprise, surprise) *The 5 Second Rule*, by Mel Robbins.

It's simple, it's powerful, and it's so obvious you'll wonder why you didn't figure it out! At its essence is the idea that if you are in the process of trying to do something (or not do something) that your brain is likely to try and talk you out of, count backwards from five and just do it. The act of counting (and in particular, counting backwards) prevents you from being able to verbalise your self-talk.

Cool, huh!

By the way, preventing your brain from verbalising is a very helpful thing in a range of other circumstances. Like getting to sleep when your mind is racing. Try counting backwards in threes from 1,000. I guarantee you. You can't do both things at once.

What we know about human memory is that there are different processes that can run in parallel – for example you can train yourself to perform visual tasks at the same time as verbal tasks (Google Stroop test if you don't believe me) but you *can't* do two verbal tasks at the same time. You can't write a coherent email and speak to someone. You can't send a text message and listen to someone (and comprehend what they said).

Knowing this can give you some quite handy insights into concentration, attention, and distraction!

So this is the psychology behind why Mel's 5 Second Rule works. Counting backwards from five actually requires some attention from your verbal processing centre in the frontal-cortex. Not a lot, but it's enough. Enough to drown out Nigel and let you get up and do the thing! And once you've started, it's a lot easier to keep going.

Second, try and find an accountability partner. Someone who you can share your plans with and get in your corner, keeping you honest and on-track.

This could be formal – like a coach or mentor – or informal, like a friend or even a random stranger you find in a forum online. It actually doesn't matter. Knowing someone else is going to ask you where you got up to with a task means you're far more likely to complete it. Even when there is no actual way for the other person to know whether you are telling the truth!

Agree a check-in schedule. It might need to be daily at first, and then move to less frequently once some habits and routines are in place. Only you can figure out what you need to keep you moving – but don't leave it to luck or willpower. Willpower is not enough. Because Nigel can influence your willpower!

Finally, the last method I'll share which is useful here, is the simple act of planning.

In the last chapter we spent quite a lot of time learning tools and techniques for planning out our big audacious goal. These techniques were mostly being applied at a 'macro' level. But the reality is, they work well at the micro level as well.

The benefit of investing the time and effort into planning well at the outset is that you are then able to break down the steps into smaller tasks... The couple of things you can do today. The few things you can do this week.

These smaller things need to be inside your comfort zone, otherwise you won't do them. If one of the tasks isn't inside your comfort zone (and you'll know because Nigel will pipe up again), ask yourself how to break it down even further. Keep chunking down until it is well inside your comfort zone, and then do it.

And life does happen. Things get busy. Family needs you. Work needs you. Be compassionate with yourself when this happens. There's no point beating yourself up. You're already doing more than most people achieve in a lifetime. Give yourself the time you need to deal with the things that pop up, and then get straight back in the ring.

The world needs you, and Nigel would very much like you to be distracted... don't let that happen!

12. Focus On Progress

"Without continual growth and progress, such words as improvement, achievement, and success have no meaning." Benjamin Franklin

There's something really daunting about taking on a really big problem and deciding to tackle it. Like seriously daunting. Like cripple-you-with-paralysis-and-fear, daunting...

At least if you aren't careful about it.

The final element in this section on overcoming inertia is simple... but not easy.

Focus on making small but discernible progress.

Because you have got this far, I know that you have created and crafted a deliberate intent to do something, and that you have visible reminders of that intent in prominent places around your home so that you keep your eye on the goal. But it's just as important that you focus on the yard right in front of you as well.

So that more detailed plan we talked about in the previous section, where you break the process down into manageable steps that are actually inside your comfort zone (as opposed to the overarching strategy – which hopefully is fairly well outside your comfort zone!)... that gets handy here too.

Each of those small tasks you've identified deserves to be celebrated when you achieve it. But here's the thing. Nigel will start trying to tell you that it wasn't important… that it doesn't count, because it was small and not that hard.

You need to find a way, mentally, to be very clear in your own mind about the connections between those small tasks that you tackle every day, and the overarching problem. And you need to celebrate your wins in those small tasks *because* they are a part of this bigger thing… not because they're small and easy.

One small thing a day might be enough. But if you have made progress – and you will make progress – then ensure you reflect on it. Notice it. Focus on it. Enjoy it. That sense of accomplishment that you will get from making one small bit of progress has to keep you going. Has to sustain you.

So extract the juice from it in whatever way you can.

I like to use the analogy of completing a large jigsaw puzzle… one of those ones where you don't actually have a scale version of the whole picture.

What do you do in that instance?

You certainly don't just start by picking random pieces and analysing them to see if you can figure out where they fit. You probably start by carefully separating the edge pieces from the middle pieces, and ideally finding the four corners. Those four corners allow you to get the shape of the thing. They allow you to create some 'imaginary' boundaries around the task at hand. And it's so clearly defined! You know there are four corner pieces (assuming of course that you've picked a rectangular jigsaw!) and you know that in between each of those corners will be a significant number of straight edged pieces, that can be readily identified as compared to the middle pieces of the puzzle.

You work away, using colour and pattern, and finally shape as the other factors to help solve the edge of the jigsaw. And while you doing this, if you're anything like me, the middle pieces are back away in the box somewhere… they aren't even on the table at this point. They aren't relevant to this stage in the process.

You set out your corners, and then you gradually fill the gaps between them, relying on colour, pattern and shape. Then voila! You have a confined box that you know the rest of the pieces will fit inside. You don't know how yet, but you know they fit somehow.

Next, (remembering you don't have the complete picture in front of you) you look at the perimeter pieces looking for an unusual or 'stand-out' colour or image. Something recognisable, or identifiable. Something that you can comb through the remaining pieces looking for.

If that doesn't work (and let's face it, there are some puzzles where they deliberately don't create useful patterns for you to work with) then you can move on to sorting the remaining pieces by colour, looking for clusters and groupings that make sense together.

Once you have these, you can start to solve that piece of the puzzle. It might only be a small corner, but if the pieces share a prominent colour or pattern, there's a better than average chance they are from the same part of the puzzle – so it is fruitful to start trying to connect them to each other.

Now you might discover as part of this process that there are further sub-divisions within the set of pieces that you've separated from the rest… there may be three areas on the image with the same colours and patterns. You just don't know until you get started. But once you start looking at that smaller part, you learn, and build your knowledge of the jigsaw. You might even start to get a few clues as to what the overall image looks like…

And you tuck that knowledge away for later, because it will help you sketch out the overall image. And importantly, it will help you figure out what elements of the jigsaw you want to tackle next.

Now this is a fairly long-winded narration of the mental processes of solving a jigsaw puzzle… but it is illustrative for a couple of reasons.

The first being that the very act of trying to solve one piece of the puzzle will help you grow a more nuanced and detailed picture of the overall image on the jigsaw. It can't not. You are handling the pieces regularly and thinking about them. Even if you disregard a piece as not relevant to your current efforts, your brain will note it and start thinking about it in the background. This is very useful.

The second is that there is a worthwhile sense of accomplishment and progress that comes from all the various stages along the way. That moment when you find the fourth corner piece. The moment when you have separated the edge pieces from the other pieces (and you hope you've found them all, but you suspect there might still be a couple of stragglers in the box). The moment when you complete the perimeter! Haha! You have all the edge pieces and it's confirmed! And so forth.

Each of these stages is worthy of your celebration. You should pause and reflect. These moments are evidence that you are on the right track. They are evidence that you are slowly but surely building and growing the skills needed to tackle the problem. And most importantly, they are evidence that you are honing your skills at sticking with a big wicked problem even though you can't see the full picture spread out before you like a jigsaw box.

What do you have to say about that Nigel!

Part Five: Impact 🦋

13. Introducing Impact

Now you might have noticed something.

We've got quite a long way into this book and we haven't actually *done* anything yet. I mean we've made plans, and thought about things, and prepared, and researched (a little) and learned quite a lot about how our brains work, and all the ways that Nigel is going to try to trip us up along the way. And that's great.

But we haven't actually done anything. Have we?

Well I have two answers for that.

The first is a quote I love…

"Failing to plan is planning to fail." Alan Lakein

The second is: you're absolutely right. The hard bit hasn't even begun yet. It's time to get started!

So welcome to the section on impact.

Why Does Impact Matter?

Hopefully, by now, this is a pretty straightforward question and you already know the answer…

The world is full of people with bright ideas and lofty ambitions… And that's great!

But if they never do anything… well that's all they are. And nothing ever changes or gets better or gets fixed or gets built or gets created or gets made, if all there is in the world are bright ideas and lofty ambitions.

I mean don't get me wrong, you absolutely need to have those things, but you need to *convert* them into actual things. Action! Impact! Otherwise they remain ethereal 'could have beens'. Regrets.

That's right. Regrets.

Many wise people have said some variation of 'nobody ever lies on their deathbed regretting the things they did – they regret the things they didn't do'. But much more eloquently than I just did.

What I'm trying to say is, having done all the work to get this far, it's vital – essential even – that you now follow through. You have the bones of a solid plan. You have a lot more knowledge than you had when you started. You have some frightening but exciting thoughts about what could be possible. And you may even have a sense of achievement at the effort and energy that you've expended so far! Great! I'm really happy for you!

But what has actually changed in the world?

Seriously. What has changed? Next to nothing.

And Nigel knows that too. He's just waiting for an opportunity to pipe up and point out to you that you haven't actually done anything yet. But he's waiting. He's waiting for a time when you're already feeling a bit disheartened, or low. A day when you're feeling anxious about how to start. A day when you're unsure about what to do next... So we now have to make sure you change that. We need to get you some runs on the board so that you can immediately answer him back and say "nonsense, Nigel!"

That's the thing about Nigel. Even though he's part of you, and you'd think he'd have your best interests at heart, it's not quite the case. He'd desperately love you to fall flat on your face... because then he can say "I told you so. I told you this was a terrible idea".

So let's make sure he never gets that chance.

So why does impact matter?

Well in some ways, it's the only thing that matters. It's the difference you make. It's the collective noun for all the changes that occur as a consequence of you being you. It's your legacy. Not necessarily in a 'remembered forever' kind of way, but in a 'sense of purpose' kind of way.

Impact is the only way you'll feel like it was worthwhile.

Impact is the only way your brain will start to feel like the effort has been well expended.

So, more than anything else, impact is essential at this point, because it will be the fuel that keeps you going, even when you don't feel like it. Even when it's hard. Even when you get knocked back (or knocked over).

Because all those things will happen, at some point along the way. And you need to be able to look around you and see how far you've come, how much progress has been made and all the ways in which you've already made a difference.

Otherwise, you'll believe them, because you'll have no evidence to the contrary.

So let's fix that.

But first, there's just one more thing we need to understand and prepare for, before we get started.

The Neurology And Psychology Of Impact

"A life is not important except in the impact it has on other lives." Jackie Robinson

So what's going on in the brain when you witness the impact you're having in the world?

The great thing about the human brain is that there are entire circuits in it designed to reward you when you do good things.

Exercise, for example, releases endorphins that reduce the sensation of pain and give you a boost of energy. They trigger the pleasure centres in the brain so that you *feel* good and have an analgesic effect, reducing the sensation of pain.

Now let's be realistic. This mechanism has nothing to do with your New Year's resolution to exercise more, and everything to do with the reality our ancestors faced… that being able to escape a predator quickly was a good thing.

Cuddling someone (and some other related activities…) releases oxytocin which prepares the brain for emotional bonding, and makes you feel good, and warm and happy. It's absolutely flooding the brain of a mother who's just given birth, but it happens when you hug anyone. Why? Because social connections were vital to our ancestors for their survival. Being ostracised by the group meant having to find your own food, and care for your own children and be on the look out for predators all by yourself. All at the same time. (It's also rather challenging to reproduce on your own…) So remaining part of a group was really important to your survival, because these tasks could be split up. One group could be out finding food while another was caring for children, and another was keeping lookout for sabre-tooth tigers.

I suspect I don't need to go into the reasons why sex makes you feel good… and you're welcome to google it if you need to. Similar principles apply.

But you can also *hack* these systems.

Certain drugs are able to replicate and trigger the neurochemicals responsible for these processes without any of the preceding activity occurring. This is part of the reason why substance addiction is such a serious issue. It really does feel good. And parts of your brain actually *believe* that whatever it is you're doing to trigger those feelings is essential to your survival.

See it isn't based on logic. It's emotional and biochemical. And your brain gets very good at doing the things that it is biologically programmed to reward. Like eating! Even when the rational, logical part of your brain *knows* it's not good for you.

So knowing this, and understanding a bit about what's going on inside your brain when you do something that makes you feel good, (evolutionarily speaking, at least) we can use this to our advantage.

To begin with, you need to think about rewards. Ways that you can trigger your brain to be happy by doing something that gets you closer to your goal (and conversely, not the things that don't get you closer to your goal). Think carrot and stick.

We're after action here, right? Not research. Not more planning. And definitely not procrastination.

Action. Actually doing something.

It doesn't have to be big, but it does have to be something.

You need to figure out how you can reward yourself for actual meaningful, impactful action. This is the carrot.

What's something you like/love/want that you could reward yourself with once you've taken action?

Ideally it shouldn't be something that sabotages anything else you're trying to achieve in another part of your life! Like having a cigarette, a glass of wine, a doughnut, or heaven forbid, smoking crack cocaine! It should be something wholesome and genuinely enjoyable. Something that will make your brain say "hey! That's great! I'd like some more please!"

You also don't want it to be something that will bankrupt you either – so a new pair of shoes or whatever it is you like to buy (for me it would be books) every time you tick something off your to to-do list probably isn't a great idea either! At least not *every* time you take action!

Maybe you could create a reward chart. They work for kids, but they work for adults as well – especially if you commit to not cheating and you involve your accountability partner in some way.

For example, you could create one of those fundraising thermometer chart things, and you could add one dollar to the fund every time you accomplished one of the sticky things on your plan, with a decent reward at the end. The visible part is important here, though. There's a reason why charities put these charts (and their more modern day digital equivalents) in prominent places! It makes you more likely to donate... So it should make you more likely to tick things off. You can put whatever reward you like at the end of it.

The converse is also true. In exactly the same way, you could take a dollar out every time you didn't achieve something you'd planned to do. Or every time you did something you aren't supposed to – like more research, or procrastinating. Make it hurt a little bit when you don't get the thing done or when you waste time on things that aren't achieving impact. This is the stick.

I'm not meaning you should beat yourself up psychologically – you're going to have days where you aren't as productive. Where a roadblock ends up right in your way. And that's OK – it doesn't mean you're failing (and don't let Nigel tell you otherwise). But you do need your brain to understand that it doesn't want to waste time. That it prefers to get that gnarly thing done. That way, you're lining up more of the dominoes to fall in your favour. You're making it easier and easier and easier to get the job done.

This is really important.

Instead of having the two parts of your brain working against each other – your rational logical you saying "what a great idea, let's do this very important serious impactful thing" and your emotional, survival oriented brain saying "arghh! That's too scary, leave me out of this, stop! Squirrel! Sabre-tooth tiger…" you can actually start to programme your brain so the two parts work *together*. Imagine if Nigel was actually pulling in the right direction! You'd be unstoppable!

And believe it or not, this is actually achievable.

Nigel spent ages telling you that you could never ride a bicycle without assistance. Then one day you did. And he saw this, and he realised that resistance was futile, and he went hunting for something else to freak out about! Nigel spent a very long time convincing you that your first day in your new job was going to be a disaster and you were going to get fired… But you did it anyway, and eventually he got onside with it! And don't even get me started on public speaking… Nigel has a field day with this one! But believe it or not, people who do it often enough gradually learn to embrace the butterflies as a sign of excitement instead of fear. And Nigel learns that the podium isn't going to collapse, you won't accidentally wander onto the stage naked, and even if your slideshow doesn't work, it isn't the end of the world. You'll figure it out. And you'll live to tell the tale!

So think now, maybe even take a minute and write a few notes: how are you going to train your brain to maintain progress and build momentum. Just like training a puppy, the feedback needs to be near to immediate, and a little bit of pleasure for doing good things, and a little bit of pain for doing bad things.

Yes, it's that simple.

What Are We Going To Cover In This Section?

Ok, this is where things get real. I'm going to share with you some very important tools for achieving impact.

There's a bit of a theme to them.

Up until this point, you've been learning how to influence YOU. How your brain works. And how it doesn't. The things you need to do to get yourself up off the couch and out of your comfort zone.

And those things are very important. Even essential. Because even if you have all the skills outlined in this section already – and you may well have – if you never leave the house to do something with them, they aren't doing anybody any good. Least of all you.

But now we have to start talking about the things that change stuff out *there*. And to be honest, most of the things that need changing are people. So this is mostly a section about leading change.

The good news is, everything you've learned about your own brain can be flipped around and applied to everyone else. Carefully.

Why do I say carefully?

Because there's a fine line between engaging people in a change initiative and manipulating people. The difference lies in motivations. If people are persuaded by the strength of your argument, the logic of your initiative, and most importantly, they agree with **why** you are doing it, they'll get onside, and your inspiration will become their inspiration – or a version of it.

This line is very very fine though. If you know someone well, and you understand what makes them tick, you *could* exploit this.

Remember when we were in the planning stages and the 'E' in smarter stood for (among other things) ethical? That applies here too.

Getting somebody to do something that they probably wouldn't really want to do if you hadn't intervened – and that isn't something they wanted to do already but didn't know how – is manipulation. And it isn't ethical. And the ends don't justify the means – this isn't a case of your goal being so 'worthy' that it doesn't matter how you get there.

Remember, Adolf Hitler genuinely intended to make life really good for the Aryan people (as defined by him). And the Aryan people, I'm sure, wanted life to be really good for them. But I'm also reasonably confident that without Hitler's intervention, we wouldn't have had concentration camps and ethnic cleansing on the largest scale ever experienced in the history of the planet.

I know this sounds extreme, but I'm really serious. This is a big deal. Let it sink in.

So what we're going to focus on are the skills you need to find your tribe, energise them, inspire them, and persuade them of the need for change, in a way that maintains the ethical integrity of the goal, and doesn't result in, or require anybody to do, anything they will regret later.

What Is Impact?

First though, we all need to be on the same page about what impact actually is. Otherwise it's all a bit academic isn't it.

To understand impact, you first need to have some understanding of the status quo. Not what is, but what the status quo stands for.

The status quo in this instance means the way things are right now. Particularly as it pertains to the field or domain where you are planning to make a difference.

The status quo, simply put, is the current state. But that can be a bit deceptive. It sounds like a very passive thing. But it isn't.

The status quo isn't a state that one person designed a long time ago and has just been hanging around for all the intervening years waiting for you to have your big idea and come along to change it.

The status quo has been 'created' – often accidentally – by a large number of people doing bold things. But the trouble is, once they've done their bold thing, they become very wedded to the results. They become invested. And when you are invested in something you become quite protective of it.

Furthermore, people who have existed within the status quo become invested in it as well – especially if they have taken any action whatsoever to defend it, even if they were 'forced'.

Let's think about this for a minute, and we'll use my big hairy goal of ending child abuse.

First, there are a bunch of people who helped create the status quo. Policy architects who designed the current child protection systems, charitable organisations who provide services to families in need or even in some cases to victims. Politicians and lawmakers who designed the overarching environment. All of them have some investment in the status quo. In other words, they're likely to try and *prevent* change from occurring to some or even all of the current system, because they have some hand in the creation of what is there at the moment.

In addition, there are a bunch of people 'content' with the status quo, who if they step into the role of defending it will *become* invested in the status quo.

A great example of this is a social worker who defends the existing procedures because they are the rules under which she must perform her job, *even if she knows* it isn't ideal. As soon as she has said to the family "I'm sorry, but this is the way we do this" she has become invested in the status quo.

In 2007 New Zealand passed a law making it illegal to smack a child, including your own. (Actually technically an amendment was passed removing 'discipline' as a defence for child abuse.) What amazed me was the number of 'good upstanding' people who were prepared to publicly defend the status quo and object to the law. In some instances, arguing for their right to discipline their own children even if that meant that other children died or were severely injured at the hands of 'lesser' parents.

So you need to understand that, even if it defies logic or rationality, there will be a great number of people who will defend the status quo and try to prevent you from making an impact.

Why? Because they've all got their own version of Nigel, and they like the way things are and don't want them to change. Because change is scary and threatening to *them*.

Or worse, because they interpret that change as a criticism of what they are currently doing (or did do). And again, Nigel doesn't like his ego to be threatened by any suggestion that he might have made a mistake.

So how does this help us understand what impact is? Impact is something you create 'out there' in the world where it can create ripples for other people.

Take this book, for example. I could think all the things I think, and I could create a system for setting my own goals and aspirations for my own life. That'd be great. But right at this minute I'm writing a crazy book. A book that has the audacity to suggest that every single person in the world has the power within them to make a small but meaningful difference. To take one problem, grapple with it, and make a real difference.

Why write this book? It's hard! It's uncomfortable! I'm fitting it in on top of my day job and raising a young man to be the best human being I can help him be… Nigel reminds me every morning at 5.00 am when the alarm goes off how much easier it would be to sleep an extra hour or so, and just get up and get ready for work, and tootle off about my day in the same way that everybody else does. Besides, he says, nobody's going to read it anyway! Let alone do anything as a consequence of reading it…

But you know what? Even if just one person does read it, and that one person does something different as a consequence of reading it, I will have had an impact. Maybe not quite the impact I'm hoping for, but an impact none the less. Impact is about creating change. In fact, in most cases, it's about leading change.

So what's involved in leading change? What are the skills you'll need to create this brave new world?

We're going to learn about:

- Mindfulness (yes, again)
- Self-awareness
- Communication
- Influence
- Marketing and Sales
- Empathy and Compassion, and
- Action

These are overlapping in many ways, but it's important to pay some attention to all of them.

So our task is to create and lead change, in the face of resistance from a range of people who are invested in the status quo. Sounds a bit like hard work. And it probably is. And the funny thing I've found is that it makes little difference what the scale of the actual change is. Small subtle changes to a system can be just as difficult as massive change. And changes to a small system can be just as difficult as changes to a massive national or global system. It's about how invested people are, and how much time and effort they're prepared to put into defending their investment. But don't worry, we'll spend a whole section looking at overcoming investment.

Although there will be times when there is someone else trying to create the same change you are, and you can hook your wagon to theirs and increase your impact. In fact you may even find that once you get started there will be a tribe of people who strongly agree with you, and hitch up to your wagon, and make the task of pulling it to where it needs to be just that little bit easier – which would be fantastic too.

Can you change the world? I don't know. I hope so. I want you to.

But what I can tell you for sure is that you will be different afterwards. And in some cases, that may be exactly what was needed.

14. Mindfulness

"We need enlightenment, not just individually but collectively, to save the planet. We need to awaken ourselves. We need to practice mindfulness if we want to have a future, if we want to save ourselves and the planet." Thich Nhat Hanh

We have talked about mindfulness before, but here I'd like to focus directly on the benefits that accrue from it – particularly the ability to notice how you are impacting the world around you.

What you do has an impact on other people.

In fact, I struggle to think of anything you can do that doesn't have an impact on other people.

Sometimes the impact is indirect. Like you're reading this book right now, which (unless you're doing it instead of something else you're supposed to be doing) might not have a direct impact in any way, but if I am even remotely successful, you will be different in some way as a consequence of reading it, and therefore, you will have an impact that is different than you would have had if you were reading somebody else's book right now. Subtle... but different none the less.

What you decide to have for dinner with your family has an impact on them. What you express to your friends as likes or dislikes has an impact on them. You have a friend who loves sushi. Adores it. You, on the other hand, can't really eat rice. It disagrees with you.

202

You're on your way to lunch and your friend suggests you try the new sushi restaurant on the corner, and before you even realise it, you say "really, sushi again?" Consequently he never suggests going for sushi for lunch, even though he would love to. And for you it was a throw-away comment because you *can* eat it sometimes, but he has now changed his behaviour as a consequence.

Our behaviour – what we say, what we do, even sometimes, what we think – creates ripples. I do this, then you do that, and somebody else does something entirely different as a consequence.

Now these ripples are not necessarily perceptible. Your friend doesn't say "I'm not suggesting sushi because I know you don't like it". So you never realise the impact of your statement. But as a consequence, the sushi shop down the road, which was already struggling to make ends meet, lays off a young woman who needed the job to help pay for her son's university study…

I'm being a bit extreme… the cause and effect isn't usually that direct, and in fact there will usually be a myriad of different things creating an impact on one system at any given point in time. I raise this just so you pause and think for a minute about the (sometimes unseen) consequences of your choices and actions.

I believe that too often we ignore these ripple effects that flow from our actions, and that this is partly why we start to believe we cannot make a difference.

The reality is we *do* make a difference. Already. Every day. You just don't know what it is most of the time.

So our first job is to start to be more aware, and more mindful of the impact we *already* have. And to think deliberately and intentionally about the impact we'd *like* to have – and importantly, to understand the gap between the two.

I'm going to introduce a new metaphor here.

I want you to imagine your leadership influence as a large bubble. Everyone has a bubble around them. At a bare minimum it takes up exactly the same space as your physical body. If you are in a space – then nothing else can occupy the same space.

Most people's bubbles are larger than their physical body though. You influence the people you meet, the places you go, the things you leave behind. The things you buy… All of these decisions and choices you make every day increase the size of your bubble in some way.

Many people are unaware of the edges of their bubble. So when they 'move around' in the world, they knock things over like the proverbial bull in the china shop. They hurt people, or damage things, or whatever it might be, but they don't even realise it's happening. They are oblivious. The cannot see the edges of their bubble, and so they cannot counteract, or correct the impact their bubble has when it interacts with other people's bubbles.

Some people have enormous bubbles of impact and are able to influence lots of people and things all the time. Like Oprah Winfrey. Oprah has a large bubble. She is able to influence many things in many ways. Even people she's never met. She deliberately chooses to use her bubble of influence in certain ways – like the school that she built for young girls in South Africa. And this influence is more than just money. She doesn't just send money to Africa to build the schools, she visits. She invests her time and energy in the girls attending the school. She passes on insights and wisdom that she has gained over the years. She is deliberately choosing to use her influence to create a generation of young women with the confidence and skills to take on the world… she is helping them to grow their bubbles – and to understand them.

The other characteristic of bubbles that is useful for this metaphor, is that bubbles are quite fragile and also quite malleable. When they are small, they naturally form more or less perfect spheres, but as they grow, they contort and bulge into all sorts of funny shapes. They can be moved about by the wind, but it is quite hard to *control* the way they move. And a sharp object can pop them as quick as a wink.

Now I don't want to take this metaphor too far – there's definitely such a thing as an overused metaphor! But I have found this a useful way of trying to understand what's going on when I try to change something. My bubble is interacting with a whole lot of other bubbles, and the results can be quite unpredictable. Which is fine if all you're doing is trying to wash the dishes, but another thing altogether if you're trying to create performance art in front of an audience…

Did I go too far with that metaphor?

Anyway, all of this is by way of saying, you need to learn to 'see' your bubble, and get very familiar with how it operates and interacts with the world.

So how on earth do you do that? It's not really there, right?

Sorry, there's no magical answer to this. It requires a bit of work, and introspection, and reflection. The closest I've come is to build a meditation practice. Every day (usually twice a day) I meditate. Just fifteen minutes a session, but the important thing is every day.

There are two parts to this I'll share. The 'how' and the 'why'.

By how, I mean what is meditation. Well, it's quite a few different things, but it basically involves letting your mind be quiet. Which of course it doesn't naturally want to do... so it wanders off. Then you notice it has wandered off (maybe quickly, maybe five minutes later – it doesn't really matter) and you bring it back to quiet. Then it wanders off, and it might be three minutes or eight minutes later before you notice. And you gently bring it back to quiet.

There are versions of this where you focus on an object or your breath when you are letting the mind be quiet. Or you cite a mantra. It shouldn't be complicated. But you need to give your monkey brain something to do, otherwise it will find things to do (and it will).

Practising meditation over time usually means you get better at noticing when your mind wanders, and therefore you spend less time wandering and more time quiet. It's like a muscle, the more often you work it, the easier it gets.

There are a few little tricks though. I've included some resources to help you get started with meditation in the book resources section of my website: www.RebeccaElvy.com/BookResources.

The first little trick is that you need to approach the whole exercise with curiosity – or at least an open mind. More importantly you need to make it a 'no judgement' zone. Those of us who are used to being high performers find meditation hard because you want to be 'good' at it. There's NO SUCH THING!

There's no magical answer. There's no perfect performance. And the purpose of the exercise isn't the exercise itself. It's what it enables you to do.

Instead, the magic happens when you *aren't* meditating.

With some time and practice, what you'll start to notice is that you begin to 'witness' or observe your thoughts *during your normal day*. Most of us move through our day with the voice in our heads (sometimes it's Nigel) narrating our thoughts as though it *is* us. But it isn't. You are not your feelings. You are not your thoughts. We hear this voice so often – in fact, most of the time – so we stop seeing it as something subjective going on inside our heads, and we start thinking of it as being what *is* inside our heads. I know that might sound a little strange, but just go with me.

Try this exercise. Pause whatever you're doing right now. Look away from the page or the screen, and take a couple of deep breaths.

Now ask yourself: "What am I going to think next?" and wait for the answer. Listen for it.

What happened?

Try it again.

What happened?

Nothing happened, did it.

You are in control of your thoughts, but you are not your thoughts.

You can think "I am an idiot" and you can think "I am brilliant". And while both of these things may be true from time to time, neither of them are who you are, or 100% accurate – and certainly not both of them at the same time. Yet the voice inside your head can be pretty convincing.

An established meditation practice gives you the insight and the mental clarity to see these voices for what they are – verbalised thoughts that occur at a point in time – and to *not* see them as defining who you are, or who you are capable of being.

And guess what?

If you are in control of what you think (rather than the other way around) why would you ever think "I am an idiot"? Wouldn't you choose to think "I am brilliant" most of the time?

So long as it doesn't start to change how you treat other people – you remain humble and generous – then it does nobody else any harm and does you a heck of a lot of good.

Anyway, this is a digression.

The point is, building a regular meditation practice enables you to start to observe your own thoughts and feelings. Rather than 'being them'. And consequently, it improves your ability to also observe the impact of your words and actions on others… and it even, and this is the really cool part, starts to assist you in observing and thinking about what might be going on for somebody else when they interact with you.

Let's say you're having a fairly challenging – but professional – discussion with somebody relating to your goal area.

The other person is reluctant to implement the changes you are recommending, and is pointing to a whole range of reasons why it won't be possible and it can't be done.

Most people (and let's face it, you aren't most people!) perceive this kind of response as an attack on their ideas and an implied criticism of everything that went into the proposals.

Naturally, a mind that interprets objections in this way feels threatened, hurt, and reacts by going into defensive mode. This usually results in going through each of the points the person raised and refuting them. Quite fulsomely.

Ultimately, this type of response usually results in an escalation of defending positions. The person you are talking to now feels they need to further defend the concerns they've raised, and before you know it, you are both entrenched in your positions, and even attacking each other.

But quite often – and we'll talk about this in more detail in the communication section shortly – the objections being raised have very little, and sometimes *nothing,* to do with why the other person is reluctant to do what you're suggesting.

But by attacking this reluctance as though it is accurate, you force the other person to defend it. And as soon as somebody begins to defend a position out loud, they become more wedded to it than they were.

The unintended consequence of this is that somebody who you might have got onside becomes an active opponent.

The trick is to get *your* ego out of the way and not to address the concerns by arguing against them, but to be open to the idea that the other person might know more about the subject than you, and ask genuinely curious questions. Be aware that what you are proposing might have personal implications for them that you cannot anticipate, and therefore the concerns they are raising are actually a smoke screen for what the person is *actually* worried about. And sometimes this personal implication may simply be (though you can't assume this) that the other person is more worried about change than you are, and therefore just needs time to get used to the idea, and even the opportunity to redesign certain elements of it.

You need to get comfortable with the idea that other people aren't like you. You might have lots of things in common. You may believe that the cause for which you are arguing is so universally accepted that nobody should be able to disagree with you. You may have mounted such a compelling and persuasive argument that no rational human being should be able to disagree with you…

But the reality is that even when we appear to be on the same page – often we aren't. And there are so many variables that go into making us who we are, that you cannot actually anticipate them all, or predict how they will all interact with each other.

So now I hear you asking "why would I bother with any of this then? If it's all a crap shoot, surely I may as well just chance my hand, see what happens and deal with the fallout in real time?"

To a point, that's exactly what I'm saying… practising meditation tends to make your more mindful – more aware of all the things that are going on in the present moment, rather than entirely ensconced in thinking about the interaction you just had with another key player in this project – or anxiety and worry about a tricky meeting you've got coming up this afternoon. It allows you to actually **be here now**.

This same mindfulness practise, once established, will also make you more accepting of, and understanding of, these fabulous human foibles we all have... The upshot of which, is that you also become better at anticipating them.

A word of caution though: I don't mean that you become better at anticipating how specific individuals are going to respond – it doesn't make you a mind reader! What I mean is that you become more adept at being open to the idea that some people will react like this, and others will react like that, and some others will react in an unpredictable fashion. And you can prepare for this. So that when individuals identify themselves as being in one of these camps, you are better able to adapt your approach and meet that individual where they are, rather than insisting they come to you.

You also need to get used to the idea that some people you encounter will respond in ways you completely didn't anticipate – even, you might say, *couldn't* have anticipated.

That doesn't invalidate their response. Your mindfulness practice – your existence in that moment with that individual will make it easier for you to figure out what to do in that moment. Which sometimes involves throwing the plans out the window and being a human being for a moment – instead of an awesome goal-achieving machine!

Now this is all well and good when we're in the abstract world of thoughts and feelings.

But you're going to be doing actual stuff, right? Taking action, creating change. Making things happen.

Unfortunately, no matter how mindful, thoughtful and well-planned you are, the actions you take – and the actions that others take as a consequence of your intervention – can have unintended consequences. Not just to the outcome you're trying to achieve, but to other people's lives.

Sometimes these unintended consequences are good things. Sometimes they feel like bad things, but ultimately they'll be seen as good things. And sometimes, they're just plain bad. For somebody.

Whether you intended them or not, you have some responsibility. You must do something.

In some cases, that will be relatively straightforward, and you'll have a chat with someone you hadn't known would be involved, or you'll put your goals to one side for a moment or two, and have a human conversation with someone… and then you'll resume more or less where you left off.

But sometimes, these consequences will force you to rethink aspects of your plan – or even the entire plan.

Again, a genuinely self-aware person can do this. It's never easy, but it is important. You need to be committed to the goal, but relaxed about the plan. Remember, the ends never justify the means.

Working through this process may cause you to make adjustments to the goal as well. You may decide that a certain component of your intended goal is now out of scope. For example, in my goal to end violence against children, I may need to alter the goal to acknowledge that the things I'm focusing on *first* won't be of any assistance for children in situations where the cause of the violence (if there is such a thing) is mental health, rather than healthy emotional regulation. That doesn't mean I don't want to fix both, but it might mean that I accept the two are entirely separate goals, that need different approaches, and that I'll tackle one first and the other second. Or I'll try and recruit someone else to tackle the second.

Mindfulness also allows you to gain insight into when you are personally at your best, at least from an energy level. Do you work best first thing in the morning? Last thing at night? Do you need to take a power-nap right after lunch to make sure you keep energy levels stable throughout the afternoon? Are you procrastinating right now?

Mindfulness helps you with all of these things. It also helps you to build resilience, acceptance, stoicism and tenacity… All of which will serve you well, no matter the project you are trying to tackle.

Mindfulness is also a necessary prerequisite to self-awareness… the topic of our next section.

15. Self-awareness

"I think self-awareness is probably the most important thing towards being a champion." Billie Jean King

Self-awareness requires mindfulness – or some version of it. Because in some ways, mindfulness is about becoming quiet enough in your own head to actually know what is going on around you – and inside your own head.

Self-awareness goes to a whole other level though.

The goal of self-awareness is to build the most accurate picture of who you are that you possibly can. And for all the reasons we've already covered, your opinion of who you are isn't necessarily accurate – nor is it the only opinion that counts! Remember, if this was a change you could create entirely on your own, then you would have done it already, right? You need other people to do things too. To change, to do something or behave in a different way from what they would have before you had this crazy idea that the problem could in fact be solved!

So what other people think of you matters. Not from an existential "oh no, nobody likes me" kind of way, but from an objective "others perceive me as pushy and opinionated" or "my approach comes across as too tentative, even when I'm absolutely convinced". These are important insights that should inform what you do and *how you do it*.

The best way I've found to visualise this is using the Johari Window. This handy tool, developed by Joseph Luft and Harrington Ingham in 1955 provides a useful way to conceptualise what we know… and what we know about what we know. And how we appear to others.

Johari Window

We want as little as possible in the unknown and blind-spot quadrants, and as much as possible in the arena and façade quadrants. The more you know about you, the more likely you are to be able to observe and anticipate the impact of 'you' on others. In other words, your job is to push as hard as you can on the boundaries so that the blind spots and unknowns get smaller and smaller.

It is important that you don't assume that other people are deluded if their opinion of you is not the same as your own. This means you won't be able to entertain the idea that it could be true. And yet in this type of thing, perception is reality. If someone thinks you're pushy, that's their reality. It actually doesn't matter whether you are. Or even whether you agree with them or not! They will interpret your behaviour as pushy simply because that is what they are expecting you to be... And remember, for them, it's all relative. You actually may be pushy... compared with all the other people they interact with on a daily basis!

Feedback as a Tool for Self-Awareness

This brings us to a very important topic. Feedback.

Now in an ideal world, feedback would come in two forms: confirming feedback that helps you understand what you are doing well, and developing feedback that assists you to modify what you are doing so you can be more effective.

But in reality, a lot of what should be feedback comes 'dressed-up' slightly differently. It tends to arrive in the form of praise or criticism. Praise and criticism tend to focus more on **you** and less on what you are **doing**. "You're amazing" is praise. "That was amazing work" is confirming feedback.

Call it whatever you like, though, you do need it. But not for the reasons you think.

I can't take the credit for any of the thinking on this – I found it in a very fabulous book called *Playing Big* by Tara Mohr, in a chapter called "Unhooking from Praise and Criticism".

As a child, assuming our upbringing is relatively 'average', we learn that we get praised for good behaviour, and told off for bad behaviour. This happens at home, when we need to do our chores and tidy our rooms, but it also happens in relation to the things we do – like making art or writing. It happens at school, our teachers praise us for doing a good job of the assignment, and they criticise or critique us when we don't. The schooling system is almost entirely premised on this approach. It starts to emerge as grades – 'concrete' things that impact us in ways beyond the relevance of the immediate assignment. Then our parents praise or chastise us on the basis of our report card... then we go to university and the basics of this model continue.

We start to believe in our inner selves that praise actually means that we are good – but worse than this... we come to believe that if we aren't being praised, that we are *not* good.

The same applies to criticism. We start to see it as being a commentary on our whole person and our whole contribution.

Failing to curtail this wrong-thinking is harmful. It can be paralysing.

Mohr argues persuasively that this affects women more than men. She does this by pointing out that girls seem to be more driven by social norms and 'acceptance' by the group's powerful members, based on an evolutionary need to belong to a strong tribal group that would ensure they were cared for and fed and protected, even if they were not as strong as other members of the group. Particularly while they were rearing children. There's some logic to this – we observe from international data collected through a range of mechanisms that girls 'do better' at school. They seem to be more adept at figuring out the rules of the system and complying with them.

Now I don't know if you've noticed this, but real life isn't like school. And it also seems that this proclivity to playing by the rules and paying careful attention to praise and criticism prevents women from being as successful in a range of non-academic domains, like entrepreneurship, executive and political leadership and so forth. It's not that they can't – it just isn't as obviously attractive to women, who seem to prioritise many other things alongside or ahead of the trappings of office.

Mohr's advice is simple. Realise that the feedback – whether it's praise or criticism – has very little to do with you, and a lot to do with the person providing the feedback.

What the heck does that mean? When someone tells you you're too pushy, it doesn't mean you are too pushy, it means that person finds you too pushy for their liking.

When someone tells you that your idea is silly, it doesn't actually mean your idea is silly, it means that they don't like your idea. There can be a raft of reasons for this, including that they're just annoyed they didn't think of it. Or that they need a bit more time to think about it. Keep going regardless. The next person might love it.

When someone tells you your idea is brilliant, it doesn't actually mean your idea is brilliant, it means that *they* like your idea! Great, that's good. But don't go thinking that everyone will like your idea. It isn't a validation of the perfectly formed nature of the idea itself, it just tells you one person likes it. Keep going regardless.

Does this mean feedback is unhelpful? Absolutely not. It just means you have to treat it with the same critical analysis you would any other data point. It's just one person's view, and it tells you useful information about what that one person thinks. You'd be wise to file that information away for future reference, because it will help you with your interactions with that person. But it doesn't mean you're a bad person, or broken, or less worthy. (Or the opposite – but only a small number of people tend to have that problem!)

So should you seek out feedback? Yes, absolutely. You should actively encourage others to give you feedback, regularly. Including (maybe even especially) from people you know aren't completely on the same page as you.

Although you're perfect, you aren't perfect, if you see what I mean. Everyone's perfect, and nobody's perfect. We all have things we can improve upon, but at any given point in time we have the capacity to put one foot in front of the other and keep moving on, regardless of what everyone says.

Those who have changed the course of history (both for better and for worse) were heretics in some way – at least to a significant proportion of the people around them.

Feedback allows you to gain insights into yourself (and your impact) that you might not otherwise have had... but only if you approach it in the right way.

In fact, there's a great deal of similarity between the way you approach meditation (openness, curiosity, acceptance) and the way you should approach your interpretation of other people's feedback.

Maybe create a little checklist of questions you ask yourself when you are thinking about a piece of feedback you have received.

- Does this person's opinion matter, either overall in my life, or specifically for this project?
- Does this confirm or align with anything someone else has said?
- Is this a different interpretation of some other piece of feedback, but with a different emphasis?
- Did I suspect this already?
- Can I do something useful with this feedback?
- Should I discount this feedback, and if I'm wrong, what would the implications be?
- What are the implications of taking this feedback on board?
- What are some alternative pieces of feedback I have received over the last while, and does this mean they were wrong? How do they relate to each other?
- Are there compelling reasons why different people's feedback should disagree?

The important thing is to keep it in perspective. It's OK to discount someone's feedback if that's what needs to happen to it. Don't forget to thank them for it anyway and, maybe if you're feeling brave, let them know why you have decided not to change your approach, but that you appreciated it anyway.

Most people don't talk enough about what is going on in their internal world (partly because most people aren't aware of what's going on in their internal world, unless they've already read this book!). Being honest is usually a good policy – especially if you need to get along with that person in order for your project to succeed.

Let's take the 'pushy' example we were using above.

Someone says you're too pushy.

You can agonise over how to be less pushy, but assuming you actually aren't, and they perceive you as pushy, but most people don't, sit down and have a chat with that person. Let them know how much you appreciate their feedback, and the courage it took for them to share it with you. That you've thought about it at length. You've even toyed with the idea of completely changing your approach, but you've decided not to, because for many people, it works, and it's true to who you are. Let them know that the reality is that you are super-passionate about what you're trying to achieve. And maybe, this is what they are picking up on, and it's coming across as pushy. Let them know this isn't your intent, and you definitely didn't intend to make them feel uncomfortable. Tell them you're going to try and take into account how they feel in your dealings with them, and that you hope that will help. Thank them again for their feedback.

If that person goes away from this interaction still thinking you're too pushy, there's not a heck of a lot you can do. But they probably won't. They'll probably start seeing it as passionate. Enthusiastic even. You'll be amazed how much just that subtle change in language will impact how they see you. Plus they'll be hard-pressed not to appreciate how seriously you took their feedback.

Please note – this won't work if you do it five seconds after the feedback is delivered! (The reasons why should be obvious... if they aren't, you may need to do some work on your self-awareness!)

The other aspect of self-awareness that's really important to mention here is that active seeking of feedback – especially from people who are unlikely to voluntarily offer it to you – can be an incredibly rich source of practical guidance on how you come across to others – both in terms of your interpersonal relating skills, but also in terms of where you are going and what you're achieving as an individual.

Now asking for feedback can be tricky, and you must only do it if you're ready to receive it.

So let's cover all of this off in a bit more detail: who to ask, how to ask, what to do while you're receiving it, and what to do afterwards.

Who To Ask For Feedback

This depends a little bit on your experience with asking for feedback and also what you are looking for, but let's assume this is new territory for you.

I'd recommend you don't start with your biggest and most active critic. While there's something to be said for 'getting it over with', if you aren't mentally prepared, and have some practice under your belt, it could do harm.

So perhaps compile a short list of people who aren't quite close friends or collaborators, but are tangentially related to what you are

Rebecca Elvy

trying to accomplish. They need to know you well enough to have an opinion – meeting you once at a fundraising event probably isn't going to cut it – and they need to be vaguely aware that you're on a mission to achieve something big (otherwise their feedback won't be well targeted).

Three should be enough.

How To Ask For Feedback

Before you approach anybody, you need to be crystal clear in your own mind about what you are looking for.

There's very little point in approaching three people and asking them to 'provide you with some feedback'. Unless they're very opinionated (and some people are) they probably won't have anything useful to offer, and they may decide not to answer at all. Giving *useful* feedback is hard, and requires a lot of thought. So you need to help them out by shaping the question/s in a much more specific way. Vague questions will get you vague answers, at best.

I'd suggest a two-phase approach. The initial request delivered face-to-face, followed up with some specific questions in written form – say via email.

This way, you aren't putting someone on the spot to give feedback in an unprepared way, but you should gain a commitment to responding to an email, and then they are expecting it, and your email won't come as a surprise.

So face-to-face I'd ask something like: "I might have mentioned to you that I'm trying to find innovative new ways to eradicate violence against children. You're a prominent activist in this field already, and I've got a huge amount of respect for you. I'm really

223

keen to make sure I'm being as effective as I can be, and I was hoping you might be prepared to offer me some feedback on my interpersonal skills and progress so far, so that I can make sure I tweak those things that aren't working so well. If you're keen, I'll send you a couple of quick questions in an email so that you can have time to think about it. Would that be alright?"

Clearly you have to tailor this to suit the circumstances. The more specific you are the better – if you can rattle off why you respect this person's opinion of you, great. If you can show them which specific area of the domain you're working in, that you're likely to seek feedback about, even better. For example, if the area you're targeting includes charitable fundraising, you might want feedback about how you are approaching potential donors and whether what they are being asked to offer, and what would be possible as a result, is clear enough.

Now the email is somewhat easier, but needs to be quite specific.

You should begin by reminding them of the conversation you had (they may have forgotten that they agreed to help you!) and then really narrow in on what you'd like to know.

You can take a couple of different approaches.

One that I like has three open-ended questions:

- What do you see as my greatest strengths in…[relevant area or field]?
- What do you think I need to work on the most in [name the area]?

- What else have you witnessed or observed that you think I need to be aware of, to be as effective as possible?

Another approach is to really zoom in on a couple of things that you suspect might be an issue for you – particularly if you've had feedback in that area before. That could look like this: "a few people have mentioned that they find me pushy. I'd love to know if you agree or not, whether you think it's an issue or not, and what I might do differently." Just be aware that for people who are less experienced at providing feedback, they're likely to respond by saying "not at all" because they don't want to hurt your feelings.

Now the entire email needs to be worded from the perspective of how useful the feedback will be to help you improve, and how much you are grateful to the person for taking the time to provide it.

Most people generally don't like providing feedback, particularly if they think either it's about an area for development: they will think of this as 'negative' (their perception, not yours) and that you might not respond well to it. We don't like to hurt someone's feelings, and we don't want to make someone dislike us. So naturally, we don't run around being completely honest with each other about their impact on us or those around them.

Your job in making this request is to make it as easy as possible for the other person to provide feedback, and to remove the risk for them. You may even want to say something like "be brutally honest – I need to know, and I'm serious about improving my approach, so sugar-coating it won't help me at all!" – this way, you've given permission. They'll probably still sugar-coat it though!

What To Do *While* You Receive It

If the feedback is delivered to your face, you need to work really hard to remain relatively expressionless – or if you can manage it, curious and open. If the party delivering the feedback feels like they've hurt you, they'll backtrack and reframe the feedback in a more fluffy way. It's human nature. So you need to approach it somewhat academically – clinically – and take notes if you can – this is quite a good way to create some space between you and the person providing it – as it means you don't have to make eye contact quite so frequently.

If you can manage it, you should ask a couple of clarifying questions along the way. This shows you're open to receiving it and you genuinely want to know what they think. The important thing is not to sound defensive.

If you are receiving it in writing, it's slightly easier.

You will be tempted to read it as soon as it arrives – that's human nature. Don't.

Make sure you are in a quiet and comfortable place – ideally away from other people if you can manage it.

Spend some time preparing for reading it. Be curious about what they have to say. Remember that it isn't about you – it's about that person's perceptions of you, from the interactions they've had with you, viewed from their lens on the world. It's not factual. It's not even objective. It's an opinion.

Armed with this pep talk, open the email and read it through. In it's entirety. Some people don't structure their written communication well, so read it right through and then start digesting what it says. Reread if necessary.

Then before you do anything else, hit reply and say thank you, you appreciate it, and you'll be in touch again in a few days to let them know what you are doing with the feedback they have provided you.

For me personally, I've created a little metaphor about feedback. I think of it as a present – a gift. Some people aren't very good at choosing gifts for people. Others are great. The existence of the feedback *does* mean they thought enough of you to give you a gift. It might be useful and practical, it might be a frippery that you have no idea what to do with, but it's still a gift. Someone put some effort and resources into getting it for you, so you want to show you're grateful, even if you decide (much later) to discard it. That's fine. But don't be hasty, and don't be ungrateful.

Now you need to spend a few days digesting the feedback. Trying it on to see if it fits. You need to be genuinely open about this – you can always decide it isn't relevant later, and that's fine, but have a go, first, at imagining it is accurate. What would it mean if it was accurate. Would you choose to do anything differently? Do other people see the same character trait as a strength? Is that trait relevant or necessary in another domain in your life, but perhaps over/under-used in this one?

Go into each element of the feedback as though it is a gift that you will be grateful for, and explore it in its entirety, before you decide what to do with it.

What To Do *After* You Receive It

Now stop for a minute. How are you feeling about the feedback you've received? Did it fill you with warmth and pride? Or was it a little bit confronting? Did it give you energy and enthusiasm to keep going? Or did it make you want to crawl up in a ball and never come out again?

Two important things are worth noting here.

1. You get to choose how you feel about the feedback you've received
2. The other person is probably feeling worse than you

Let's deal with the first one for a minute.

Remember how in the last section we talked about mindfulness, and how it lets you objectively observe your thoughts and feelings? Well this is where that comes in super handy. A solid mindfulness practice should allow you to witness your reaction to the feedback – both the 'good' *and* the 'bad' bits, and then decide how you are going to use it to your advantage.

This could be as simple as recognising that it is how one person sees you, and not an objective truth about how you *are*.

Equally though, you might recognise a kernel of truth, and deeply reflect on how you might incorporate this new knowledge into your approach in the future. Verbal communication – in person or in writing – is never perfect. You cannot assume that the other person's words came across to you exactly how they meant it to, but you *can* assume that they were trying very hard to convey an important point that they wanted you to take on board. Now you have to decide what you are going to do with that information.

Second, if there are elements of the feedback that are cutting (or frankly even if there aren't) chances are pretty good that the person who took the time to provide you with the feedback is worried about how you've taken it.

Likely they are feeling a bit awkward about it. And may even be avoiding you because they're worried about what you're going to say in reply.

So it's up to you to make the first move and bridge that gap. I'd suggest you use the same format as the feedback was provided in. If it was in writing, reply in writing. If it was face-to-face, set up a meeting. But make sure you prepare thoroughly beforehand – you might still need to write your reply anyway, just to make sure you don't miss anything.

The purpose of this is as follows:

- To express gratitude to the other person for taking the time and making the effort to provide you with feedback
- To provide them with a couple of insights into what you are doing with the feedback, ideally one insight that relates to a positive element of the feedback and one that relates to a negative or 'constructive' element

- To invite that person's help with one of the actions you've decided to take – maybe holding you accountable, pulling you up if you slip, or reconvening in a few months' time to see if you've been successful in implementing the desired changes
- To ask clarifying questions if an aspect of the feedback wasn't immediately obvious to you
- To offer to reciprocate if they ever want feedback or support of a similar nature
- To thank them again for their generous assistance.

All of this goes to the prime point that you should treat feedback as a valuable gift, that can either help move you forward or stop you from progressing... the other person meant it to be the former. The rest is up to you.

16. Communication

"The single biggest problem in communication is the illusion that it has taken place." George Bernard Shaw

Communication is a powerful tool. It's also exceedingly error-prone and fraught with difficulty.

In fact, when you think about it, it's a wonder that human beings have survived as long as they have without annihilating themselves… (and you might argue we're in the process of doing that as we speak – but enough of the doom and gloom!)

Human beings are often distinguished from other animal species for our ability to communicate, and in particular, the richness of human language – both verbal and non-verbal.

In this section, I'm going to try to impress upon you the power of communication as a tool, but also highlight some of its massive fallibilities, and what you can do about them.

We'll also spend some time talking about communication channels. What are they? When should you use them? Then we'll explore understanding – the desired goal of communication.

I'm not sure how or why, but I have an uncanny ability to 'read' people. Particularly their oral communication. I've lost count of the number of times that I've been in meetings with very senior and successful people where they clearly are talking past each other, and neither of them realise it. Like, seriously completely oblivious to it.

It's only afterwards as agreements unravel, or deliverables don't meet the other party's expectations that they start to see that what they thought was agreed, wasn't. And in every case, both people think the other is at fault and that their recollection of how the meeting went (and what was agreed) is flawless and the other person is being deceptive or mischievous.

Seriously, I've seen it over and over again. And while I usually try to intervene, there are many instances where it has been my boss – or my boss's boss, so I often tried to work behind the scenes to bridge the gap before the inevitable train wreck.

And these are clever successful individuals! Not recent school-leavers, or children, or people working in entirely different domains… these are people who arguably should be able to understand each other.

It happens with family members a lot too… there's a reason why big family gatherings are often fraught with controversy and tension!

Now this observation is incredibly intangible. So for a while I wasn't sure if I was just imagining it. But over time I've come to trust it, because it has proven to be valid time and time again. I've also learned to speak up as quickly as possible, because often the damage is done once the parties leave the room. If either side goes back for clarification – and the stakes are high – it risks looking like reneging on what was agreed. That's never a great position to be in!

I think the effect I'm referring to is often exacerbated if the parties are on opposite sides of an 'argument'. Particularly negotiations, but essentially any time where the parties aren't speaking frankly… they're trying to be subtle or clever, or not reveal their entire hand. But also if there's a power imbalance and one person doesn't want to come across as overbearing, or the less powerful person doesn't want to give away too much.

All of this is to say that, even when the stakes are incredibly high (I'm talking multi-million dollar deals – in some cases hundreds of millions), oral communication is fraught with error. Not subtle error, but completely missed the boat error. Different ballpark error. Not even playing the same sports code error.

Given talking is something that most of us have been doing since we were toddlers – and listening even longer – why is this the case? We've had a *lot* of practice! We've survived high school with its pubescent innuendo and emotional experimentation. We've had good educations, where these things were taught. We've studied the classics of literature, read widely and witnessed countless real and fictional conversations on television and in the movies... Why can we not actually understand other people very well?

To figure this out, the first step is to take a very close look at the inside of your own head.

Thinking.

Now, hopefully at this stage you've started to build a meditation practice, so you've got a better handle on your own thinking than most people, but still. We need to take a bit of a look.

Thinking happens entirely internally. While it's true that your mind usually verbalises it for you – an internal monologue of sorts – you experience this monologue within a multi-dimensional array or memories, anxieties, anticipation, and emotion.

If for example, you are thinking about a meeting you'll be having later today, not only will you be mentally rehearsing what you want to say, but you'll probably be remembering similar meetings you've had in the past (and how they went) you'll be thinking about the people who will be attending the meeting, and what your experiences of those individuals have been like (did you have a run-in with Bill in the lunchroom the other day?). You'll be imagining the outcome of the meeting, and what you want to get from the meeting. In addition, you might be thinking about what you've got to do immediately before the meeting to be properly prepared. You might be thinking about the consequences of this meeting – getting it right, or getting it wrong. But the feelings are really important. You'll be thinking about how important the topic is to you. You'll be thinking about the connections between this work and the organisation's strategic direction, and therefore how important it is that everybody is on the same page from the outset. You'll be excited and anxious, and worried, and maybe even elated about the outcome (your brain is quite good at enabling you to anticipate feelings that you might have in the future – for some people this is anxiety, and for others it's excitement and hope).

As you can see from this, what goes on inside your mind when you are preparing for a meeting is a rich tapestry of thoughts, feelings, and emotions. Positive and negative. Relevant and irrelevant. Factual and imaginary.

Why does this matter?

Well this fictional meeting we're referring to here is not unusual. This multi-dimensional quality that accompanies your thinking is present pretty much every time you think.

Now as you prepare to communicate, depending on how high the stakes are, you start mentally rehearsing how you will 'say' the thoughts in your head. But compared to your mental universe, verbal (and non-verbal) communication is a pretty low-fi substitute for thinking.

You have to find the right words for a start.

Do you know how many words in the english language there are to describe emotions? Dachar Keltner, author of *The Power Paradox* carried out a study where they analysed the responses of people to emotionally charged video clips. They identified 27 discrete emotions, but what he and his colleagues learned was that there are actually some 'pairings' of binary emotions where you can 'feel' somewhere along a graduated line between the two! This means there are far more emotional states than 27... and just as many words to describe them.

Yet most people only use a very narrow vocabulary of emotions to describe how they feel – to vocalise how they feel.

The counterpoint to this is that there are feelings you have but can't put into words – because you don't have a word for it. That feeling can never be adequately described. I'll give you some examples (from other languages) courtesy of ThoughtCatalogue.com :[*]

---

[*] https://thoughtcatalog.com/brianna-wiest/2016/02/40-words-for-emotions-youve-felt-but-couldnt-explain/2/

Altschmerz

n. weariness with the same old issues that you've always had—the same boring flaws and anxieties you've been gnawing on for years, which leaves them soggy and tasteless and inert, with nothing interesting left to think about, nothing left to do but spit them out and wander off to the backyard, ready to dig up some fresher pain you might have buried long ago.

Pâro

n. the feeling that no matter what you do is always somehow wrong—that any attempt to make your way comfortably through the world will only end up crossing some invisible taboo—as if there's some obvious way forward that everybody else can see but you, each of them leaning back in their chair and calling out helpfully, colder, colder, colder.

Adronitis

n. frustration with how long it takes to get to know someone—spending the first few weeks chatting in their psychological entryway, with each subsequent conversation like entering a different anteroom, each a little closer to the center of the house—wishing instead that you could start there and work your way out, exchanging your deepest secrets first, before easing into casualness, until you've built up enough mystery over the years to ask them where they're from, and what they do for a living.

We tend to have a set of words we use often... a verbal signature if you like. Chances are your family or colleagues know these quirks. They expect them of you, so they notice if something is amiss.

So let's assume ideal conditions – you are in the meeting in question, you've prepared mentally for what you want to say, and nobody interrupts you, or distracts you. You use some words to portray your rich inner world to your colleagues...

At best, you portray the bones of your conceptual ideas and the weight of your feelings about them...

Then everyone else in the room repeats the process in reverse – they take the words you actually used (provided they were *really* listening, and not just waiting for their turn to speak) and they process them in *their* brain, which has another set of emotions, and cues, feelings and thoughts. Ultimately they arrive at what they *think* you meant.

The chances of it resembling – even remotely – what you *intended* is so slim it's quite frankly a wonder we get anything done as a species.

It's why other people's behaviour is so often mysterious and unpredictable. It's why we fear delegating responsibility to someone else. It's why team work is so hard.

I made this point earlier. You basically take a rich hi-fi concept, convert it into a low-fi substitute in the form of words and (if face-to-face) gestures and intonation, transfer it through the air in the form of waves to a low-fi receiver in the form of another person (who has to be actually listening in order to take it in) and then they transfer those low-fi words – plus their own interpretation of your gestures and intonation – into hi-fi thoughts and feelings and concepts inside their own brain. Fool-proof!

It improves slightly if you know the people you are communicating with. Think about the feedback process we referred to in the previous section. If you know that somebody you need to communicate with tends to see finger-pointing as threatening (whereas you like to point for emphasis) you'll hopefully know not to point your finger to illustrate your argument.

Email and other written communication is worse – you remove the ability to use intonation and body language, and suddenly your words are being entirely misconstrued. Never use email for complex discussion. Call first. Stop by and deliver it face-to-face. Follow up with email… But don't let email do the talking.

Now it's possible that in the not too distant future we'll develop technological aids to communication that enable us to accurately portray the emotional and conceptual components of our thoughts to other people. There are people and organisations working on it as we speak. But until then, the best you can do is be as clear as you can, avoid ambiguous phrases and words, and accept that only about a third of what you're trying to get across will arrive at the intended destination, so you'll need to compensate by asking follow-up questions, seeking clarity through further discussion and iteration, and even then, assume that the other person might not understand the full depth of your feelings on the matter.

Furthermore, the other person might choose not to ask questions, even if she realises she doesn't understand what you are saying. We are inherently wired to avoid conflict. You also don't really want to hear a dissenting view... because it challenges your worldview. When you combine these two things together, the likelihood is that the things you *most* need to hear are also the ones that are *least* likely to be raised with you.

Here's a question for you.

Who is responsible for understanding? The person doing the understanding or the person conveying the message?

In an ideal world, you'd say both, right? Two people enter into a discussion about a topic they both have some interest in, and they persist with the discussion until they're 'on the same page' for certain.

Has that ever happened to you?

My experience has shown that generally the person conveying the message uses the 'standard' version of the message they always use, and the other person either has no idea what you're talking about but doesn't want to appear stupid, or assumes they understand your meaning and goes off to do their interpretation of it.

I remember one day I was sitting in a café doing some work when I became aware of a couple of men at the table next to me. Their conversation was quite loud, and one of the men seemed to be expressing a great deal of frustration. Not at the other guy, but at people in general.

I gleaned he was a sales rep of some sort – possibly an insurance broker. It seemed the second guy was either a coach/mentor or a friend. It was hard to be sure because he didn't say much.

"...But then they go to the competition, and they say it's on the basis of price, but don't they understand I'm getting them a discount of 60, 70 sometimes even 80 percent off the standard retail price already!"

His frustration was evident, and it was obvious that he felt betrayed by his disloyal customers.

I remember being struck by the absolute conviction he had that he was right, and his customers were being ungrateful and unreasonable.

And then it struck me that he'd almost certainly never told them the discount he was obtaining for them. Or made it clear how much work he did on their behalf to obtain that discount. Or how much he valued their business.

To be honest, he was quite probably off trying to secure the next *new* client, and not really making his existing clients feel particularly valued or special.

I remember leaving the café thinking about the responsibility for making sure that someone understands.

Really, the only answer is, the person responsible for ensuring that understanding occurs is the person who actually cares that it occurs. Sometimes that will be the person imparting the information and sometimes it will be the person receiving it.

In an ideal world, both people would take equal responsibility for ensuring that there was common understanding, but the world is seldom ideal.

These issues are compounded by factoring in how many people the message is being delivered to. If you are talking with one person face-to-face – or even a small group – you have the ability to observe their body language, respond to their questions, ask clarifying questions to see if they have understood and so forth. This potential is lost when you are talking to a group that numbers in the hundreds, the thousands, or even the millions.

Hopefully by this stage you are gaining an appreciation of just how complex interpersonal communication is.

But there's still one more complicating factor to add into the mix... channel. We have an increasing array of communication channels available to us... yes, there's still the standard face-to-face or in writing – but those can be varied hugely by the medium in which they are conveyed. Digital or analogue? Live or recorded?

The exact same message you used on Instagram won't work on Facebook. A video recording can capture a lot more than a sound recording alone. A handwritten note says something entirely different than a template email, even when the words are identical.

You need to be mindful of not only what your message is, but how it is delivered. And the meaning of that channel to the people receiving it.

Dumping your girlfriend via text message says something quite different than dumping her via a carefully handwritten note. Versus broadcasting it on Facebook.

So how can you improve your communication skills? You've got the information now, but what can you actually practically do differently to be more effective in getting your point across – especially when it matters most?

Awareness

Being aware of the shortcomings of human communication is a good start. That awareness will enable you (combined with your new mindfulness practice) to be much more deliberate and intentional about what you say and how you say it. You'll be able to assess the stakes more clearly, and play through, in your own mind, the potential consequences of *misunderstandings* and whether those consequences are serious or merely frustrating.

Purpose

Be deliberate – don't leave your critical communications to chance. Don't rock up to the meeting or the presentation without being comfortable that you've taken all the steps you need to on *your* end to increase the odds of successful communication occurring. You know who's in the room, and what they're likely to be most concerned about. If you know someone in the room takes a while to warm up to new ideas, you've spoken to them separately in advance. If you know the topic being discussed is technically complex, you've prepared some useful supporting materials to make it easier to understand. You've thought about what time of day would be most effective. You've thought about ensuring you have the right people in the room. You've even thought about the venue. Is it comfortable? Is it conducive to the discussion going well? Does the room create an unhelpful power differential? For example, it's in the boss's office, which could mean people are less likely to speak up.

Delivery

Accept that you are responsible for this message all the way up to successful receipt and understanding at the intended destination. That includes all the facets of the message's delivery, but also the customer care afterwards. Follow up. Did it have the intended impact? Has it been understood? Has it been passed on accurately? Choose the right medium for delivery, to increase the likelihood of success.

Repeat – But Not Identically

If you remain unsure that your message has been received and understood, repeat it, with slight variation. You might hit the mark this time. Or it might be the other person needed to hear the message a couple of times for it to sink it. That's fine. Put in the effort – the added clarity it's likely to bring is to your benefit. And the added effort that is exerted in responding to misunderstandings if you don't will exceed it every time, so it's generally time and effort well spent.

There's a rule of thumb in marketing… that someone has to hear a message (about a new service or product that might benefit them, for example) seven or more times before it will register as something they should act on.

The brain sees novelty as scary. Remember Nigel and his fear of new things? Every single person you're trying to persuade has one… A little voice inside their head going "oooh, that's different, I don't like that. Let's just keep doing what we're already doing, that's safe, right?"

By repeating your message multiple times in multiple ways, with slight variations, you can start to normalise it. It gradually becomes something that already exists, rather than something new. And the more time that elapses without the world ending, the more likely it is that Nigel will relax just enough to actually listen to what you have to say. The time this takes is different for everybody. And it isn't your job to wait for *every* body. Just enough to help you gain momentum and start moving forward.

Practise

This probably seems obvious, but unless you're delivering a keynote speech to hundreds of people, we live in a world filled with instant gratification: with livestream video and selfies, and off-the-cuff remarks. Sure, this creates engaging content – it can be raw, and personal, and flawed.

But how likely is it that it conveys the exact message that the 'speaker' intended?

Probably pretty low, actually. If there was an intended message at all.

Regardless of whether you are giving a speech, recording a video, or trying to be persuasive within the context of a meeting where you aren't the chair, practising beforehand is important. Ideally with someone who understands the topic a little, and the context a lot.

Anticipate

Without over-analysing, spend a few minutes thinking about the ways that what you intend to say could be misinterpreted.

In an organisational context, this often means deliberately thinking about other people's motivations and fears.

For example, if what you have to say creates some change from the status quo, consider who might 'perceive' this will impact them negatively. I say perceive, because it doesn't matter what the truth is. You might be proposing something that will have long-term benefits for everybody, but I would still put money on there being somebody who sees change as scary and thinks they will lose their job, or get moved from their comfortable office to a big scary open-plan seating arrangement, or have to share their lunch break with someone they don't like... or whatever. And while you can't be expected to anticipate *all* of these things – and to be honest, some of them won't have much reality to them – the act of anticipating them is incredibly useful to creating the possibility of a 'generic' objection that you can at least acknowledge in what you say. Just be careful not to come across as dismissive. For the people having them, they are valid concerns.

Be Clear About Who You Are Talking To

If there's some controversy around the subject you are communicating about, hold very clear in your own head who it is that you are trying to reach.

There are probably three broad 'camps' of people: those who will be with you/the proposal; those who will be against you/the proposal; and those who haven't made up their minds yet.

Don't ever fall into the trap of spending your energy trying to win over those who will be against you or the proposal. Speak to the people who are already with you, and the people who are sitting on the fence.

You can certainly acknowledge that there are some people who won't like the idea – and leave space for them to get back on board by saying something like: "I know that this sounds a bit scary, but I'm happy to speak with anyone who has questions, and I know that once you start to see the results in a few weeks time, you'll understand why I'm suggesting this."

Again, this isn't actually for the people who are against you. There might be some who take you up on it. But it's actually for those who are sitting on the fence. It starts to inoculate them from being pulled into the negative camp by those members. It provides them with evidence that you are reasonable, and a reply to those who say that it's being rushed, or not thought through, or the rationale is unclear – they can say: "well, why don't you go and speak to her if you have these concerns."

Don't Take It – Or Make It – Personal

When you have a big idea that you think is amazing, it's really easy to feel personally responsible for that idea, and to 'own' it as something you created. That's natural. People are invested in their ideas and so are you.

But that also makes it less about the idea and more about you. Which can create its own challenges.

For example, it makes it very hard for you to engage in genuine dialogue with the people around you, in a way that could change or modify the idea. Doing so will feel to you like a personal attack or criticism of you, rather than the idea itself. Instead, set it free. If it's a good idea, it will find its own voice/s in the organisation.

Likewise, don't make other people's distrust or criticism of the idea personal about them. It might be, but keep to the topic – talk about the idea, while mentally allowing space for the fact that there may be no way to amend the idea to meet that person's needs. But focus on the idea, not changing the person! That's a long hard row to hoe!

Be Flexible

As the debate and discussion evolves, you might find that someone else comes up with a brilliant idea that isn't simply an improvement on yours, but something entirely different, and better.

If you have your eye clearly on the end result you are trying to achieve, that big audacious goal you set earlier, you'll be able to spot this, check it's alignment with the objective, and recognise that it's a great idea, and worthy of jumping on board with. The sorts of change and improvement you're seeking in the world aren't about ego or taking the credit. The result is what matters.

Feel free to suggest improvements, obviously, but don't be so wedded to your own idea that you become blind to other, potentially better, ideas that would get you to your goal faster.

Also, often there's room for more than one big idea!

Build Ownership

We're going to talk about influence and persuasion in a later section, but bear in mind that the more people see the idea as 'yours', the *less* they care about it. The more they see it as theirs, the *more* they care about it.

Try and think about ways that you can build ownership, which is basically just a jargonistic way of saying, help people realise that the idea is good, by coming up with it on their own, if you possibly can.

People who are helped to see the scale of a problem, and build enough dissatisfaction with the status quo, often come to the solution in their own time. And when they get there, they are far more committed to making it happen than they ever would have been if you simply presented them with the answers.

Encourage Dissent

It can be very tempting to think that people disagreeing with you is threatening the validity of your idea, and therefore bad for the overall achievement of your objective.

But if your idea is good, if it is strong and has potential to make a difference, it will stand on its own. In fact, if it is good enough, you will quickly get other people advocating for it, without you needing to do anything.

So don't be afraid of dissent. For some, that's their way of 'road-testing' the idea. The people who Edward de Bono would term "black-hats". People who enjoy the idea of trying to kill an idea by poking holes in it. But these same people will ultimately become proponents of the idea if they are allowed to work through this process, and come out the other end seeing that the idea still stands. Often they become the strongest advocates. Remember, for people like this, it is entirely about the idea itself. It isn't about you, or them.

(OK, it's a little bit about them). But they genuinely want to kick the tires and make sure it's roadworthy before climbing on board. That's not an unreasonable desire.

Communication has many, many flaws. We're not nearly as good at it as we'd like to think we are. We frequently cross wires with others, and even completely misunderstand what each other is saying.

But there are a range of things you can do that increase the odds in your favour. They make it more likely that the essence of your message is communicated effectively to the people you most need to hear it, and even in a way that they can immediately take action with it.

Unless you are able to single-handedly affect the change you are seeking in the world, you need to hone your skills, and become a confident and effective communicator.

Accept you won't get it right every time (even forget the idea that there is a 'right' way to communicate) and embrace communication in all its messiness as the single best way of transmitting your idea to someone else.

It might even be the only way.

17. Influence

> *"Think twice before you speak, because your words*
> *and influence will plant the seed of either success or*
> *failure in the mind of another."* Napoleon Hill

In many respects, everything we've covered so far is leading up to this point.

Influence.

It's one of those terms that's bandied about as though it is bestowed upon you by others… social media influencers, influential business leader… And to an extent, people can objectively and externally gauge your influence by the impact it has. But that isn't the whole story. Some of the most influential people in our society today exert their influence entirely behind the scenes… most people don't even know they exist!

Part of me would love to distinguish between these two examples of influence by referring to them as 'overt influence' and 'covert influence'. But that makes the latter sound a bit shady, and to be honest, either approach can be wholesome and ethical or dodgy and worthy of keeping behind closed doors! So I'm not sure it helps us here much at all.

Anyway, influence is about convincing somebody to do something differently than they otherwise might have because of you – your persuasion, your example, your leadership. Influence can be direct or indirect – and as I alluded to above, it can be positive or negative.

For example, blackmail is a form of (illegal) influence. Threats of physical or psychological violence are a form of influence. Equally, competitions with the lure of a big cash prize or a trip are a form of influence. So is appealing to somebody's goodwill (exploiting their guilt) or taking advantage of someone's naïveté.

The reason I'm covering it in this book is that influencing other people is likely to be crucial to your plans. From persuading your spouse or significant other to support your efforts to join the Board at your local school, to persuading politicians and policymakers to endorse and support your petition to parliament or congress. Influence is required for all of these, and everything in between.

I cannot think of an example of a large and ambitious goal or objective where influencing others isn't necessary to some extent – even if it's just to obtain the emotional support of your family while you carry out the work. That is still influence.

At its heart, influence is about getting into somebody else's head (or several somebodies) and making the task more about them than it is about you.

Unless you're incredibly charismatic, it's rather unlikely that somebody is going to do something just because you asked them nicely (although that does work sometimes). What you need to be able to do is tap into what might make the other person want to do that task for themselves. Of course it's not possible to completely separate these two things out, but you have to think about "what's in it for them". Why would they do this thing? What about doing it might make them feel good? Or respected? Or virtuous? And what emotion is it that the other person is craving to feel? A sense of belonging? A sense of contribution? A sense of being accepted and part of a team?

I suspect you can see why I included the 'e for ethical' in the SMARTER goals definition earlier on.

Con artists and cult leaders are exceptionally skilled at influencing others. Although, they tend to focus their energy on people who are susceptible to their charms in the first place.

For our purposes, I suggest you need to think of influence as a tool of leadership – and a true leader doesn't require anything of someone else that they wouldn't be prepared to do themselves. Or ask their mother to do. (Unfortunately this caveat might not rule out cult leaders or con artists, who have been known to include their own mothers, and likely would be prepared to do these things themselves provided they were the beneficiary!)

Really, your job when it comes to influence is to figure out what information the person needs in order to reach the decision you want them to reach on their own. You want them to retain the ability to choose. Otherwise it's less about influence and more about coercion.

I'm relying on you to be morally upright and good about this, because I can't possibly list the dos and do-nots in a helpful or readable way. Manipulation is bad, and I trust that you picked up this book because you're motivated to do good. Remember what we discussed earlier – the ends don't justify the means. The actions you take to achieve your goal need to be consistent with the goal, otherwise it's sullied and undermined. You've got to own your impact, and redress the unintended/adverse consequences of your actions as best you can. Be driven by love. Not ego or fear. And do no harm.

So what is influence? In essence it requires the following things:

Clarity Of Purpose

This goes straight back to your inspiration, your 'why'. You need to be able to articulate this clearly to someone who isn't you. Somebody who doesn't 'get it' yet. Somebody who's given you five minutes of their busy schedule because you asked them 17 times in a row. Somebody who has their own 'why' and their own priorities, and their own causes, and their own commitments and concerns and worries.

You may also have to be able to articulate it to someone whom you're meeting as a representative of an organisation or group. This adds complexity, because now you have two sets of everything I just listed to worry about. It's fairly rare (unless you're talking to the founder of the organisation) to find a situation where an individual's motivations and priorities are *identical* to the organisation they represent.

Clarity Of Required Action

You also need to be crystal clear about what you are asking the other person to do. There is no room for ambiguity here. It's OK to have some 'hope they might do these things too' things, but you need one crystal clear unambiguous cogent action that you want the other person to take. The one thing that if they do nothing else, you'd be happy.

It could be an introduction, it could be a donation, it could be a sale – it doesn't matter, but it needs to be so obvious that the other person cannot misunderstand your intent.

Research

Now before you run off thinking 'got it, can't wait to get started', you need to do your homework. How much do you know about this person? How do they think? How do they make decisions? Who are their stakeholders? What legacy are they trying to create? What constitutes success for them? Are they a detail person or a big-picture/conceptual person? Are they always rushing and want you to talk fast, or will they let you take your time?

Now the answers to these questions (and any others that you come up with as being relevant to your purpose) might not be readily available, but some of them will. Has this person got a social media profile? Have they written a book? What jobs have they had in the past, and what might that tell you about how they think and work? Do they have an assistant? Because if they do, assistants often know more about their bosses than their bosses know about themselves! At least the great ones do. And while they're not likely to reveal the family secrets, they might be able to give you a few pointers like whether the person will be rushing straight into another meeting, whether they have any sympathy for the issue you want to discuss. Some assistants can even 'warm-up' the person you're meeting with before you get there, but be careful of this. The assistant probably won't be as passionate as you are about the topic, and this could also cause harm to your purpose by colouring the person's judgement of what you are doing before you even step into the room.

Find out what you can, make some 'safe' assumptions based on what you learn, but remain ready to adjust your approach in real time, if you realise that it isn't hitting the mark.

Message

Once you're clear about your message, your action, and you've done your research, you're ready to craft your message. Think elevator pitch. But don't stop there. It's possible that your elevator pitch will be so great you get to keep talking. So make sure you have a rock solid elevator pitch that speaks *directly* to the person you're speaking to. It can't be generic. Don't just rehash the pitch you used for the last meeting. Adjust the length, the emphasis, the proposed benefits and so forth to match what you learned about the person you're speaking to.

Write it down and rehearse it. You need to know it so well that you can move it round, play it backwards, and repeat/rephrase as necessary to get the point across.

When you're as passionate as you are about the topic, this shouldn't be as hard as it sounds. Just remember that your passion may not be matched – if the other person isn't an overtly passionate person, remember that it probably won't help you to increase your level of enthusiasm in the hope that it's going to be contagious – this seldom works, and in fact can really turn some people off your message.

Rapport And Chemistry

Once you've crafted your message, you're as ready as you'll ever be to deliver it. Now you need the stars to align… No, it isn't about luck. It's about building rapport. Be genuinely interested in what the other person is doing, what's going on for them. If they seem distracted, offer to make an alternative appointment. Add value. If you see a way that you can help them, offer it. Without being greasy.

In an ideal world, your relationships have already been built before you need to make this kind of appointment. But sometimes that's not possible. Be ready, though, if it's clear that someone isn't warming to you, that you might be better off going more gently and building the relationship more before you ask for their help.

If you are concerned that you aren't well endowed in the charisma stakes, I'll say two things. First, being passionate, committed and taking the initiative are all very 'charisma-enhancing' qualities, so don't undersell yourself. Second, make sure you read *How to Win Friends and Influence People* by Dale Carnegie, and consider employing a coach or mentor in this area if you really are concerned. It might be someone who can help you with speaking more assertively, presenting with confidence, public speaking, presenting data and so on – so be really clear about what the area is that you think you need some help with – go specific not general. It really helps having someone objective giving you some pointers.

Be Observant

Be alert for cues and signs from the other person that you need to adjust your approach. Don't stick to the script at the expense of adding value or strengthening the connection.

I have this very profound memory from an Organisational Design programme I took at Columbia University. We were working in syndicates and we had to prepare for a meeting with a fictional client called Mr Lomas – our task was to 'sell' him our consulting services in organisation design. There were three of us. We were ultra-rehearsed – even scripting who would say what, how we would handle questions and objections and so forth. About two minutes into the conversation 'Mr Lomas' (played by the fabulous and very capable Dick Axelrod) said "well that's all well and good, but the unions are on my case, I can't even get the current negotiations sorted out…". Now it happened that this is an area of professional expertise for me. So I acknowledged and empathised… but pivoted straight back to the purpose of *our* meeting. Forward-looking transformational change.

He turned us down.

Why? Because he had a real problem. Right now. And we could have added phenomenal value by solving that problem for him. Right away. If we had pivoted our offering to include or be front-ended by using that process of industrial bargaining to gather the data and insights we'd need to assist with organisational strategy, we might have walked away with a six-figure consulting gig.

I've never forgotten this salient lesson.

Trust

Many people find trust a difficult concept to grasp. I like to think of it like this:

- Do what you say you will do
- Treat people the way you'd like to be treated
- Help others with no expectation of receiving anything else in return
- Express gratitude when somebody helps you
- Say sorry when you make a mistake
- Don't betray a confidence
- Make sure your actions match your words

Trust isn't about grand gestures or heroism. It's about the accumulation of many small interactions. And the fabulous thing about trust is that it works like relational lubricant. It makes transactions and interactions easier and faster. It's also easy to shatter and hard to repair – so treat it very carefully.

For more on trust, read *The Speed of Trust* by Stephen Covey Jr.

Targeted And Tailored Communication

We've mostly touched on this already, but avoid vanilla.

It's easy to do vanilla. It works for most people most of the time, but it's not exciting. It's not memorable. It's safe. It's easy to forget. Yet virtually every ice-cream flavour worth having has 'vanilla' as its base… you can embellish vanilla without too much risk of creating a cacophony of flavours that don't go well together.

So you need to *start* with vanilla. That's your elevator pitch, and your longer spiel… but you need to be ready to embellish. You need to tailor your message to suit the tastes of the person you want to swallow it.

Maybe I've taken this metaphor too far… but ice-cream…

Call To Action

You need to include a very clear request. Unambiguous. "It would be really helpful if you could do x. I know that's a big ask, but it will assist this project to get off the ground and gain some real momentum…"

It needs to be explicit and precise.

Commitment

But you don't get off scot-free here… you should be prepared to offer something in return. Ideally something that exceeds the value of what you are asking for (in the eyes of the other person).

Draw on your personal skill sets, or the work the project has already delivered, or the connections you have… You'd be surprised at what you can offer someone when you really think about it. If you can't think of anything on the spot, you can also ask and offer. "Is there anything you need that I could help with?" Sure, they can say no. But the offer was there.

In addition, you should not be afraid to seek *their* commitment. You've gone to the trouble of preparing for this meeting and going through the discussion – you've presented your case. Don't forget to close.

Follow Up

This is not a case of set and forget. You need to follow up. Send a handwritten thank you card. Or a small gift.[*] Actively engage with adding value for this person and the things they care about.

Also, follow up to ensure they do what you need them to do. Not in a rude way – just in a courteous, is-there-anything-I-can-do-that-would-enable-this-to-happen kind of way. You might be surprised at the small obstacles that get in people's way sometimes – make it your mission to remove those obstacles if at all possible.

Now, you may well be reading this and thinking to yourself "this sounds a lot like sales…". Well, you'd be right.

It is. It is *exactly* like sales – irrespective of whether you are asking for money, time, connections, products, publicity, support, endorsement… it doesn't matter. You're asking for something. And you should expect to offer something of greater value in return.

The best sales reps in the world genuinely believe that the product they're selling is worth much more to the people they're selling it to, than the price-tag. They're genuine about helping and adding value.

The worst sales reps don't care whether the client needs the product, they're just after the commission.

---

[*] Just be aware that a lot of organisations rightly have policies that prevent their employees from accepting gifts. This is to avoid the appearance of, or actual, conflicts of interest… which ultimately lead to corruption.

So long as you place your intent, your actions, and your follow-through firmly in the first category, you need not feel bad about 'sales'. Too often, we associate 'sales' with shady used-car salesmen. But the world is full of sales that don't follow that model – embrace that.

18. Marketing and Sales

"I have always said that everyone is in sales. Maybe you don't hold the title of salesperson, but if the business you are in requires you to deal with people, you, my friend, are in sales." Zig Ziglar

Now, I'm going to be completely honest. This is not my strong suit. But I will teach you what I know, and I'll try and connect you with people and resources that might be useful.

So I see it like this. 'Sales' is basically another word for providing value to somebody else. It might be in the form of a product or service, but it could be in terms of an idea or concept or knowledge. And it's sales, because there is generally some form of exchange. That exchange might not be money – all that matters is that both parties agree the value.

It is this exchange that economists argue led to specialisation of labour and trade. If I'm really good at growing grain – that's easy for me. But apples – they're hard work and need far more time and attention than I can spare. But you – you're great at apples. You eat, sleep and dream about apples. Apples are a cinch. Grain on the other hand…

So my grain is worth more to you than it is to me. And your apples are worth more to me than they are to you. So we have a little chat, and we agree to exchange a certain amount of grain for a certain amount of apples. Both of us are happy, because we feel that the amount we've given away is worth 'less' than the amount we've received in return. It's a genuine win-win.

Marketing is nothing more than letting people know what it is that they could buy in exchange for something they already have.

Is this an oversimplification? I don't think so. Many people find selling 'icky'. But if you really believe you are providing something of value – value that exceeds what the customer is offering in return – then the other person feels like they got an amazing deal – what's there to be icky about?

The real challenge is in valuing your ideas appropriately – not too much (artificially) and not too little – and figuring out what you can offer to others in exchange for something that you need. When you are passionate about the end result, and you connect that result to what people are doing in a way that resonates for them, the rest becomes much easier. In some instances, the rest simply takes care of itself!

Focus more on the other person than you do on yourself. That's probably the key to all of this. The more you can take 'you' out of the equation, the more success you're likely to have. Everyone is thinking about themselves – so if you think about them too, you're more likely to connect. So long as you are clear in your own mind about your final destination, it will keep you on the right track… you don't need to be so focused on you. Don't worry, you won't get lost!

For me, I've had a number of sales (or combined service/sales) roles – particularly early on in my career. This experience has served me well… should we say, it has been 'sufficient' till now. But by the same token, I'm very aware that I prefer to share knowledge when it comes to providing value. I struggled when I was selling products that I had no hand in creating. And I witnessed time and again the extent to which sales reps are swayed by their relationship to the firm making the product or the percentage of commission they receive for it. Often both. This is more in line with the icky sales I referred to earlier. I think you only need to look at the extent to which pharmaceutical companies 'woo' doctors and healthcare professionals to be a bit worried about this effect. If the product was that fabulous, surely it would speak for itself?

But unless you're big-pharma, you probably shouldn't be too worried that this is what you're doing.

Dan Ariely has some fabulous examples of this in his book *The Honest Truth About Dishonesty.*

Marketing is all about taking this insight – that it's not about you, it's about them, and writing/speaking in a way that really convinces somebody else that they need what you're offering.

If the orchardist with the apple farm doesn't know you have grain available to sell, he might take all his apples to the market down the road! And if he thinks that there's no difference between your grain and that of his neighbour, he might get his from there instead. It's about honestly, but persuasively, closing a knowledge gap. Correcting assumptions, and addressing information asymmetry.

But most of all, it's about explaining the value of what you have in terms that matter to the other person.

And it's almost entirely about emotion.

As Simon Sinek would say, "people don't buy what you do, they buy why you do it".

If your inspiration – your 'why' – is strong, and it came through strongly in the way you speak about what you are asking for.

Even though your why almost certainly isn't the same as the other person's 'why', they'll recognise and respect yours. It will speak to them on an emotional level. It will connect – deeper than just words.

On its own, though, that might not be enough. You also need to make some educated assumptions about the other person's why. How might your 'why' speak to their 'why'.

Based on what you can observe of this person – the choices they have made, the public statements they have made, even the way they greet you. Where they work, what they do. If they are a founder of a company or charity, you can expect there to be quite a lot of alignment between their why, and the why of the organisation. But even if they aren't the founder, unless they are deeply unhappy in their job, there will be some alignment between their 'why' and something the organisation they work for does or believes.

Think of it this way. When you've been job-seeking, have you ever seen the perfect job – you're qualified for it, it's interesting, doing something that you love – but then you see who the employer is... the name of the company... and you think "No. I could never work there." Or you have gone to work somewhere, and a few months in, you start feeling 'out of place'? Like you won't ever feel at home there?

The technical term for this is lack of 'values alignment'. In other words, things that are important to you, that you hold dear, are not the same as what this organisation says or does. Consequently, you don't feel like you're pulling in the same direction.

On the other hand, when your values *are* in alignment with the organisation you work for, going to work is a breeze. You can't wait to get up in the morning. It's exciting. You feel like you have a purpose. That you are fulfilled. That you are contributing to something bigger than yourself.

For these reasons, you can make some relatively safe assumptions about the other person's 'why' based on the fact they work for a certain company. At least to a point.

So as you are preparing for the meeting, be aware that you are entering into a transactional relationship. This isn't just a casual chat. You want something. The other person probably wants something. And you don't know yet exactly what it is... part of your job is to figure out what it is, and see whether you can arrange it. If you can't, you may know somebody who can.

Your job, in essence, when you realise that someone else needs to do something in order for you to be successful, is to make sure that person will choose to do the thing you need them to do. To make sure that what you want and what they want are in perfect alignment – even if it is for entirely different reasons. You play the translator. You enable other people to see how the things you need them to do help them achieve *their* goals – either directly or indirectly.

Be creative! There's lots of scope for it. When the challenge you are trying to accomplish is this big, there are many many ways to get there. You have the inspiration. You have the intent. Now you just need to make the impact.

19. Empathy and Compassion

"When you show deep empathy toward others, their defensive energy goes down, and positive energy replaces it. That's when you can get more creative in solving problems." Stephen Covey

Achieving impact is almost impossible if you lack empathy and compassion, assuming the impact you are seeking involves some other person or people.

The world we inhabit is full of people. Other people. People who aren't exactly the same as us.

People who can look different but think in similar ways. People who can look the same, but who think entirely differently. People who share our values and aspirations, and people who don't. People who are ambitious, and people who aren't. People with too much and people with not nearly enough.

Our psychology is very finely attuned to the need to create social in-groups and out-groups. From the very early stages of cognitive development, children start building the tools to figure out whether someone is 'more or less' like us.

From the way our brains process vowel sounds in spoken language, to our ability to recognise* the faces of our immediate and

---

* There is actually a dedicated area in the brain for recognising faces. If it is damaged, you can lose the ability to recognise faces. It's called the fusiform gyrus, and prosopagnosia is the medical term for someone who has an

extended family, our brains become exceedingly skilled at quickly figuring out whether another person is 'in' our group. Or not.

It's a sad truth that a white European child will be skilled at discerning faces from his or her own ethnic group, even being able to tell apart identical twins, while *not* being able to distinguish between someone of, say, Japanese descent and someone of Chinese descent.

It is likely that our baser tendencies towards racism stem from these cognitive shortcuts, though aren't excused by them. Our primitive ancestors had very minimal chance of bumping into someone from an entirely different continent while popping out for a bottle of milk. In fact, it was likely to be more useful for our ancestors to be able to tell the difference between two different sabre-tooth tigers who patrolled the surrounding mountains than it was to be able to tell the difference between someone from India and someone from Sri Lanka. Or New Zealand and Australia.

Yet, we are all human. DNA sequencing suggests that the percentage of our genetic makeup that differs from person to person is so small – 0.1% – as to be almost a rounding error. Yet here we go, making smaller and smaller fine-grain distinctions between different people – based on inane things like hairstyles, or fashion sense, or religion, or whether they own the right kind of car, or a car at all…

Now for a while empathy was the virtue-de-jour that every leader should have to be effective. But many researchers and

---

impaired ability to recognise faces – sometimes not even able to recognise their own face.

academics felt it was getting a bit of a bad name. The general interpretation of empathy is 'the ability to walk in somebody else's shoes' and *feel* how they feel.

I don't know any leader – professionally or otherwise – who can do that consistently and not get completely worn down by it. Spending too much time feeling everybody else's ups and downs is a sure fire path to emotional exhaustion and burnout.

Besides which, there's a sort of selfish arrogance, that comes from assuming you can *feel* another person's pain or elation. It's theirs – not yours. Internalising somebody else's feelings as your own almost seems to me to deny them the uniqueness of their own experience.

Have you ever had someone say "mmm, I know how you feel..." when you are going through something really earth-shatteringly painful or traumatic? And the worst part is, that statement is usually followed up with "*I* got fired once..." or "*I* got divorced once..." or "*my* dog died once..." and a story about the *other* person. How does that help you? You don't want to know that 73 million other people were fired across the globe this year, this is *your* experience, right now, and you want a little bit of time for it to be about you. Not too long, mind you. No wallowing. But enough time to extract some important experience out of it. To learn from it. And to find your own narrative so that you can move on.

Of course there'll be a point – hopefully in the near future – when realising that this experience, that seems tragic and overwhelming right now, is actually mundanely commonplace and generally people get through it OK, will be incredibly valuable. But other people are terrible at knowing when you've reached that moment. Sometimes even *you* won't be completely sure.

So for these reasons, empathy has tended to get a bit of a bad rap.

The preferred response now is compassion. This is a much more selfless response. The focus is on the other person. You can respond with things like "how can I help?" or "what do you need right now?" or "would you like to talk about it?". These are all more generous and have the potential to lift the other person up in a way that focusing on your own version of a 'shared' experience never can.

Part of the issue, though, is that people seldom need you to be at your best most compassionate self at a time that fits *your* schedule! It's usually inconvenient. Often you're right in the middle of something. Or heading into another meeting. Or about to make a vital phone call.

The other thing that makes it tricky is that many people aren't very good at letting you know they are looking for compassion. They don't come to see you with a sign that says "Seeking Compassion". They pop in to ask you about something else. Or they make small talk about the weather, or the game on Saturday.

Blink, and you'll miss it.

Remember Mr Lomas from the last chapter? He was in a kind of 'professional' pain, and I missed the opportunity to be compassionate... and the business walked out the door with him.

All people are human. All people are worthy of your compassion. Generally people are doing the best they can with the tools they have.

Make that your mantra.

You can't know exactly what sort of day someone has already had. But you can choose whether you make it better or worse. Choose better.

20. Action

"When it is obvious that the goals cannot be reached,
don't adjust the goals, adjust the action steps."
Confucius

The world is full of people with big ideas and no follow through.

It simply isn't enough to plan and plan, and strategise. Nothing will get done unless you *do it*. Nothing will change unless you *make it happen*.

Nigel, on the other hand, would like you to believe that planning is at least as good as doing – if not better! Because it's safe. You can't really tell whether you got it right until you put your plan into action – so if you never put it into action you can live blissfully unaware of whether it was a great plan… or not.

Now, and this is important, you don't need to know every single step between where you are and where you want to be. You only need the next few steps. That's it. A few steps. Once you've taken one or two of these steps, the next ones will become obvious. It's like the scene in *The Labyrinth* where Sarah, Ludo and Hoggle are trapped in the Bog of Eternal Stench. Ludo summons the rocks, and the next ones appear in the Bog at just the right time for everyone to step their way across the swamp without stepping in the foul murky depths.

"Faith is taking the first step even when you don't see the whole staircase." Martin Luther King, Jr.

This is really important, because it requires an act of faith. Or supreme confidence. Use whatever word works for you, but either way, you are taking the first steps without knowing exactly what the few steps are after that. Or after that. It would be easier to keep planning. Of course it would. Nigel would be happy. In fact deep down, for a little while at least, you'd be happy too. You'd be warm, and safe, and comfortable. You wouldn't make any mistakes. You wouldn't be embarrassed, or corrected or ridiculed. It would be great!

Except nothing important ever got done that way. And you want to do something important.

So let's talk about taking action.

We've spoken already about how powerful laziness is. It is evolutionarily beneficial. The difference between those who survived and those who didn't was directly related to your ancestors' ability to conserve all energy that wasn't strictly required for hunting, avoiding being hunted, and – well – making more people.

That's no longer the case. We consume far more calories than we need to stay alive, and we can always get more if we need them. So get up and do something. Be mindful of how you are spending your time, and develop an **action orientation**.

Action Orientation

You know that saying about how if you want something done, ask the busiest person to do it? Become that busy person. Deliberately and intentionally develop an action orientation disposition. Describe yourself as someone who gets things done and makes things happen. If necessary, take a look at how you spend your time now. If you're not sure, try keeping a time log for a week[*]. Then make an honest appraisal of whether that time was well spent or not.

Before we go any further though, I want to make one thing absolutely clear.

Spending time doing relaxing things you love and spending quality time with your family and loved ones and friends, *is* time well spent. It's vital to your psychological and spiritual replenishment. You will not achieve the big audacious goals you've set if you don't deliberately create time to do those things. I am not suggesting that those things are lazy, or able to be reduced.

However. If you are spending an hour veging on the sofa watching Netflix and not actually connecting with your family, take a look at *that* time.

If you disappear into your Facebook newsfeed for an hour at a time, and wonder where the time went afterwards, take a look at *that* time.

Deliberately identify the times you will work towards your goal. Schedule time explicitly for that purpose. Draw on your

---

[*] There's a template in the resources section of my website www.RebeccaElvy.com/BookResources

accountability buddy, if you have one. And use that time wisely. Even if it's just one hour a day, you'll be surprised at how quickly those hours add up into something substantial. And equally how easily they disappear if you aren't intentional about it.

It is often as simple as being sufficiently mindful (remember that meditation practice you started earlier!) to ask yourself this question: "Is this the best use of my time right now?"

"Is this the best use of my time right now?" So simple. But it really works.

You define best use. That's the greatest part. But don't lead yourself astray. If you've done your prioritisation and planning work well, and you're clear about how your family and leisure time stacks up in that mix, you'll easily be able to answer it. Going on a date with your spouse or significant other – yes. That's the best use of my time. Playing games with your kids – yes. That's the best use of my time. Correcting my best friend's punctuation on Facebook – no. Not the best use of my time.

It's a deceptively simple question, but if you can find the right places to insert it into your inner narrative, you'll find you eke out time during the day you didn't realise you had!

Coping With Setbacks

Things aren't always going to work out the way you want them to. People will say no. Some people won't 'get it'. Sometimes you'll fall off the productivity bandwagon and waste a whole weekend catching up on your personal social media. While none of this is ideal, it's OK. Get back on the horse, as the saying goes. Whatever you do, don't let Nigel do his "Oh well, there's no point then" routine. Because he'll try.

Any time you give him an opportunity, he'll pounce on it. In fact, Nigel piping up with a few low-blows is usually the sign I use that it's time to take action and get a few things done! He tends to be more vocal when he thinks I'm not making any headway – so that should be a trigger that I need to take a look at whether I'm keeping up with my action orientation!

Now nobody – I mean nobody – likes to be 'rejected'. In fact we've created this special word for it. Rejected. It sounds so final and even fatal. (It's one of Nigel's favourite places to attack you when you're down!) But the reality is, rejection is just somebody else saying no.

Can you possibly imagine a world where you could say 'yes' to absolutely everything somebody else asked you to do? The busier you are, the more successful you are, the more you have to guard your precious time. Saying yes to everything simply ensures that the squeakiest wheels – or the quickest requestors – decide what your priorities are. And when everything is important, nothing is.

But remember, the one thing we all have in common is the number of minutes we have in one day. It doesn't matter whether you're Warren Buffet, Tony Robbins or the homeless person sheltering in your local main street. You have 1,440 minutes every day. And so does everyone else.

You should be spending them consciously. You should know where they go. Ideally, you should be spending them on paper before you spend them for real. And sometimes, you'll need to say no to great opportunities because you already had plans for those minutes.

The same is true for other people – particularly the kinds of busy and effective people who will be able to assist you with achieving your goal.

When they say no, they aren't saying your idea is bad. They aren't saying you're silly or stupid for pursuing it. They aren't saying you should give up (though that's not what Nigel will say). They're simply saying they had other plans for those minutes already.

There's nothing hurtful or dangerous about that.

Remember our fear of rejection stems from our ancestors' dependence on their tribal family for survival. You aren't in the same position. I'm not saying you shouldn't be disappointed. That's human. But you can't let it get you down or stop you from keeping on. It happens. That path has closed down. Double back a few steps and take the next path. And the next path. And the next path.

Successful sales people (the sort who deal with rejection *a lot*) know that being told 'no' doesn't hurt them at all. In fact, most of the really great ones will tell you they'd rather hear a very prompt and forceful "no" than be led along for an hour and a half by someone who has no intention of buying but wants to be polite!

Develop a thicker skin. Accept that a certain number of 'nos' are part of the journey. In fact, make it your mission to get them over and done with as quickly as possible. And then move on.

Setbacks come in other forms too. Sometimes you'll be wrong. Just plain wrong. In spite of all your research and analysis, in spite of how big and fabulous your brain is. In spite of how pivotal this piece of information is to your hypothesis of what needs to happen for you to solve this problem. Sometimes you'll just be wrong.

For some reason (and there's a theory that suggests our schooling system is at least partially responsible for this), we're conditioned to see failure as a bad thing. As something to be avoided at all costs.

Consistently, research into successful entrepreneurs and innovative companies finds that willingness to fail – and to fail often – is key to their success.

You can't wait till everything is perfect before you try it. We've all heard that Thomas Edison took 10,000 failed attempts before he achieved a functional incandescent lightbulb, and when asked he said "I have not failed. I've just found 10,000 ways that won't work"*.

This is all about mindset. And the great thing about mindset is that you're in control of it. Provided you can keep Nigel quiet. You decide how you define failure. And more importantly, the attitude you take to it when it happens.

Instead of ruminating about how bad it is, try asking yourself what you can learn from it. Try drawing inspiration for what to do next time. By all means ask some great questions and extract valuable information from it. But that information shouldn't be

---

* The exact quote is very hard to track down. The best I've found is: "I have not failed 10,000 times. I have not failed once. I have succeeded in proving that those 10,000 ways will not work. When I have eliminated the ways that will not work, I will find the way that will work."

emotional in nature – it should be factual. It should be objective. It should be quasi-scientific.

Efficiency, Effectiveness And Multiplying Your Time

We've spoken already about being deliberate with how you spend your time… But there's slightly more to it than that.

If you are serious about accomplishing phenomenal things, you need to not only focus on efficiency and effectiveness, but you need to be looking for ways to invest your time so that you 'earn' time tomorrow, and the next day.

This concept comes from the book *Procrastinate on Purpose* by Rory Vaden. He describes how efficiency is doing things well. Effectiveness is doing the right things. But the real secret to productivity (if that's even the right word for it) is doing things today that mean you can free up time for something else tomorrow. He encourages people to start thinking about ROTI – Return on Time Invested.

For example, every month, you get a bill from your utility companies. Water, electricity, whatever it is. And you open the bill. Read the bill. If you're attentive you might spend a little time comparing it with last month, or even this time last year to make sure it seems 'about right'. You procrastinate on it for a bit. Then eventually you go into your bank and pay the bill.

With the advent of modern banking though, you can now set up your payments to happen automatically! Sure it takes some time to set it up, but once it's done, you don't have to do it next month. Or the month after that. Let's say it normally took you 30 minutes to pay your bills every month. And imagine that it took you one hour to set up the automatic payment authority (and it probably wouldn't take that long). Two months down the track, you've 'paid' back the initial investment, and every month thereafter, you have 30 minutes you didn't have before.

Most people don't think about time like this. It's why most managers are terrible at delegating. Is there ever a good time to teach one of your team members a new skill? No. Is there ever going to be enough time to coach them through the first few times when they forget, or get it wrong, or you still need to go through it carefully to ensure it's done to your standard? No. But a few months down the track, when that person – feeling newly empowered by your expression of trust – is kicking arse at doing the thing you taught them to do, you'll be making back the time invested and more besides.

It's kind of like compound interest. There's always a bunch of fun things you could do with your money. But get it into an interest bearing investment and you start earning interest. And then interest on interest. And then interest on interest on interest... The sooner you start, the higher the return on time invested. Remember, there's never a convenient or perfect time to make the investment – but the sooner you make it, the sooner you'll realise the returns and be able to use that time for something even more beneficial.

Not everything can be done this way though. There are some things you just have to do. For these, do spend a little time trying to ensure they are as productive – as efficient and effective – as possible.

If you must attend that networking event tonight, and you're really not looking forward to it, because it seems a waste of your time, try and turn it to your advantage. Set yourself the goal of trying to find someone who might be interested in what you're working on. Try and hone an interpersonal skill you struggle with, like remembering names. Gamify it – I'm going to introduce myself to 10 people I've never met before.

Think a bit outside the box as to how you can turn more of your time into productive time. See your recharge time as active productive time, rather than 'wasted' time. It will make you feel more effective. You'll gain momentum.

Ask Great Questions

Finally, when it comes to taking action, the most important thing is to be sufficiently mindful (or deliberate) that you can ask yourself the right questions at the right time. I know we've talked about this before, but it's so important it bears repeating.

Every morning you should be asking: "What one thing can I do today that would really move the needle on this project?" Sounds simple. But remembering to ask yourself a question is hard. Even printing it out and putting it somewhere prominent isn't fail-safe – things that you see often become 'invisible' to us within a very short space of time. Have you ever driven home from work and then realised you've arrived in your driveway, but you have no recollection of all the intervening distance travelled?

Your brain simply blanks it out because it's familiar. There's no novelty. No risk. And therefore nothing worthy of paying attention to.

You have to bring what mindfulness experts and practitioners call "a beginner's mind" to the exercise. The deliberate ability to approach something as though you've never done it before.

The fabulous thing about questions is that your brain hears the question and immediately starts looking for the answer. This is why the question has to be open and empowering. There's no point asking yourself a question with a yes/no answer. There's not even much point asking your brain questions that begin with who, when or how, unless what follows it is something you don't already know the answer to. What is great. What can I do...? In what ways do I need to think differently...? What other approaches could I try? What can I learn from...?

As I said earlier, it is absolutely OK (in fact it's vital) that you spend time on just being. Relaxing, recuperating. Recreation is an important aspect of a healthy mind, body and soul. This book is not about saying you must spend every waking moment working on something significant and noteworthy. It's about ensuring that you are *deliberately and intentionally* choosing how you spend your time.

It should never be a case of "oh, darn, I just spent an hour playing Candy Crush". It should be something you choose to do before you do it. Something you choose to do with full knowledge of why you are doing it *and* what you are choosing *not* to do in that exact moment.

If you aren't *intentionally deciding* what to do, Nigel will do it for you. Any ideas yet what Nigel would like you to do? Hint: It isn't changing the world!

Learn to be aware of what you are doing. Learn to intervene in your own decision-making so that you have some input, rather than being an innocent by-stander.

Make your moments count. Not because they all need to be equally significant, but because you have a finite number of them, and collectively you want them to add up to something.

Part Six: Overcoming Investment 🦋

21. Introducing Investment

> *"Attachment to the past and fears concerning the*
> *future not only govern the way you select the things*
> *you own but also represent the criteria by which you*
> *make choices in every aspect of your life, including*
> *your relationships with people and your job." Marie*
> *Kondo*

You're probably thinking "what on earth does investment have to do with achieving massive results in an area I'm passionate about" or words to that effect.

Good. I'm using investment very deliberately here. I'm referring to the tendency that human beings have to become increasingly committed to something they've worked on closely[*]. Emotional investment in a project, if you will. Not financial investment.

A slightly less charitable way of looking at this is the fact that we human beings don't like to admit that we might be wrong. The more effort, energy and emotional investment you put into something, the less likely it is that you'll be able to turn around later and say "hmmm – that might not have been the best idea after all."

This matters here for two reasons.

First, there's your own investment. You were inspired to do something to fix a problem you saw in the world. You sat down and nutted out what could be done about it. You took massive action. You're well down the path to achieving the thing.

But now you're invested. If the plan wasn't working, would you be able to see it? Would you be able to accept it? Would you be able to walk away and start from scratch on a new plan?

The answer is, only with great difficulty. Don't worry – that's normal. That same investment is the power and energy that gets you up every morning with a sense of purpose, that you're on a mission. You just need to be aware that it may be blinding you to the effectiveness of your plan.

The second reason that investment matters here is that you aren't alone in being invested in things. People all around you – including those with influential roles in the exact area you are trying to exert change – are invested in their own vision for change *or* the status quo. Their own version of Nigel will be telling *them* that change is

---

[*] This is sometimes referred to as the IKEA Effect – by the time you've spent hours pouring over those hard to follow, poorly translated instructions, you're going to be pretty attached to your new coffee table!

bad, and consistency is king, and that what *you're* trying to do is dangerous and jam-packed full of sabre-tooth tigers.

Your Investment – Stubbornness

The human tendency to value something more highly if we have had a hand in creating it, is both fascinating and sometimes counter-intuitive. Economists find this particularly perplexing, it's yet another example of irrational behaviour from human beings who should be able to rationally decide how best to spend their energy and resources. Economists would argue that the moment you realise something isn't working – it isn't likely to work out the way you thought it would – you should stop 'investing' immediately. Everything you have already invested is a sunk cost. You can never get it back, but throwing more good time and resources in the pit after bad isn't sane or rational.

And they're right. Kathryn Schulz has written an important and intriguing book called *Being Wrong*, in which she explores the human tendency to insist we are correct, even when evidence shows the contrary.

Interestingly, a willingness to be wrong – to fail – seems to show up consistently as the primary differentiator between people who succeed as entrepreneurs and everybody else. An acceptance that success requires consistent failure. And that it's better to fail quickly, learn from it, adapt and move on than to persist in flogging a failing idea.

Yet knowing this intellectually, and being able to *see it* when it happens to you are two entirely different things.

For this reason, it may be advisable to include, as part of your weekly or monthly review process, a deliberate and explicit consideration of the question: "is this working?". Are you getting the results you expected? Is the resistance you are experiencing expected or extraordinary? Are you comfortable with the level of investment you have made to date. Will you still be comfortable if it takes twice as long again? Or three times? What would happen if you walked away today? Are you comfortable persisting in the way you have been, for as long as you think it will take, only to discover that you've made not one iota of difference? And importantly, what could you tweak or change to increase the likelihood of success? You may find putting an end date on the activity in question helps – if you haven't succeeded by that date, you change tack.

Your Investment – Lack Of Persistence

Now because we human beings aren't already complicated enough, history is also littered with examples of people who persisted for quite a while… and then abandoned hope just days, or inches, away from the major breakthrough they were seeking.

Napoleon Hill in *Think and Grow Rich* tells the story of a gold miner who did everything right – figured out where he thought a rich gold seam should be, invested in the right equipment, prospected like crazy, then eventually gave up just a few feet from the seam he correctly predicted would be there. Needless to say, the guy who came after him had a much easier time of it!

So please don't think that I'm telling you you'll need to walk away. I'm not trying to do that at all. In fact, the opposite.

All I'm trying to do is alert you to the fact that there will be a line between persistence and over-investment. That line will be obscured with a litany of evidence in both directions. Your job is to obtain sufficient mental clarity at regular intervals during the implementation of your plan – ideally with some pre-determined off-ramps along the way – so that you can make logical and informed decisions about when it might be time to double down *or* call it quits, rather than emotional ones.

Other People's Investment – Resistance

Because your plan is big and audacious, it is highly likely that it is going to intersect with other people's plans. Or other organisations' plans. You might recall that earlier, when we were talking about Impact, we had a brief introduction to other people's version of Nigel. This is where he (or she) tends to show up.

There can be all sorts of reasons why other people may have plans that aren't in alignment with yours, and it isn't always obvious why. In fact the plans you 'bump into' may not have anything to do with your purpose at all, which therefore makes them very hard to anticipate. Other people's motives aren't always clear.

More often than not, other people aren't even sure of their motives themselves. They just know that they 'don't like' something. In the same way that I expect there's been a few things in this book that you hadn't been fully aware of – particularly about how your own brain works, and how you think, most other people don't know those things either. They don't notice their own thoughts, they aren't aware of their own motivations, and they often aren't conscious of the impact that their actions have on others.

Organisations can be a little easier to predict, but it's important to remember that organisations are basically made up of a whole lot of people, any one of whom may not 'like' what you are doing, and may hold sufficient influence in that organisation to obstruct your plans.

As I mentioned earlier,[*] one of the most challenging jobs I've ever had was cleaning up after a very poor IT implementation between an offshore vendor and a government agency – neither of whom was *actually* the end-user of the software service being implemented. Unbeknownst to the client, the vendor had made a decision very early on in the tender process that this particular implementation would be a loss-leader so that they could gain a 'toehold' in that country.

Now of course, as you might expect, they never disclosed this to the client. (Though perhaps one could argue it should have been obvious by the price they quoted!)

Deciding up front that something is going to be a loss-leader, and then actually 'stomaching' that loss as it hits the company's financial position and share price, are two quite different things. So the *financial* investment necessary to ensure that the service would be successful and 'world-leading' was not sustained or sufficient.

Once the implementation went wrong (and oh boy, did it go wrong), the prospect of the 'toehold' in the market place vanished in a puff of smoke. Consequently not only had the company made a slightly unwilling but *accepted* loss in developing their solution,

---

[*] You'd be forgiven for thinking I'd only ever had the one job. No. It was just so rich with examples of what *not* to do that it's hard to beat when it comes to drawing on my own experiences!

they also realised they weren't going to make any return based on securing further clients.

Needless to say, their willingness to spend more money to fix the system was next to zero. The reputational harm had already been done. The company moved into loss minimisation mode...

Now this sounds very logical and rational for a company. And that's true. But remember that their client is a government agency. One that is not accustomed to thinking in such a 'mercenary' and commercial manner.

In fact, an organisation that believed that failure was not an option – that the political and reputational fallout of failing to implement an easy-to-use and accurate system was intolerable, and consequently was prepared to persist and persist with development and implementation even when there were warning signs that things were not going to go smoothly.

Talk about a clash of 'investment'!

From everything I have been able to discover, the client never imagined that a vendor would accept a loss to gain other business without disclosing that at the time of tendering for the business. It also never occurred to the client that the vendor could consider just walking away. And certainly that the vendor could ultimately care so little about fixing the problems that arose due to the shortcuts that had been made along the way.

To be fair to both parties, the real failing in all of this was the complete lack of trust and the massive (and in some instances, deliberate) information asymmetry between the parties.

But it serves to illustrate that you can only know what you know, and you will unearth resistance to your plans that will seem unfathomable within the paradigm you are using to guide your thinking and actions. But the same will apply in the other direction – the person 'resisting' you will find your ideas equally confounding and alien to their worldview. Never underestimate the level of investment most people (and organisations) have in the status quo!

I'm not suggesting you need to spend a lot of time anticipating all the possible permutations of this – that's not practical. I am suggesting that by being open to the possibility that this can occur, you increase the likelihood that you will recognise it quickly, and find a way to move forward, or manoeuvre around the resistance, or whatever might need to happen.

There are basically two types of resistance: your own and everybody else's...

22. Procrastination – Overcoming Your Own Resistance

*"Procrastination is like a credit card: it's a lot of fun
until you get the bill." Christopher Parker*

Resistance from you – your own resistance – tends to come in the form of procrastination.

Now procrastination is a bit of a sneaky beast. It can pretend to be all sorts of other, less sinister, things. Usually Nigel has a hand in this.

Life gets busy, or a little bit of self-doubt begins to creep in, and suddenly it's far more important to organise and tidy your office area, or to re-alphabeticise the spices in the pantry or to vacuum, than it is to make that phone call.

Now there is an extent to which knowing these tasks are complete may help you relax and be more productive. But equally, I will state for you categorically: there is NEVER a perfect time!

Once the spices are re-ordered, you'll find something else that needs to be done. Because the cause of the deferral isn't the lack of organisation in your kitchen. It's something about the task you should be doing instead... Drawing on your newly acquired mindfulness skills, try and notice this feeling and recognise it as a signal there is something that needs your attention.

Feeling Overwhelmed

Many people, myself included, tend to procrastinate when they aren't sure how to do the task they face. It feels big and a bit daunting, so you put it off. Anyone who has written a university essay will relate to this one! It usually means you defer starting until the last possible minute. I mean the last possible minute when it is still physically possible to complete the assignment before the due date.

The consequence of this is that the entire task gets truncated into a few hours, when it probably warranted a few days (when you include research, planning and review). You ultimately hand in a more-or-less completed essay, but you know deep down that it's not your best work!

In my view this is partly to avoid being disappointed (if you worked really hard and didn't get the 'A' you hoped for). It's much better to put in a half-hearted effort and be surprised by a great grade or not surprised by a mediocre grade. After all, you hardly put any effort in!

It's amazing the lengths your brain will go to, to justify your actions in retrospect!

When you break a big (or daunting) task down into its constituent parts, though, you make the whole thing seem more manageable. Especially if you can then spread it out over a number of days.

- Day 1: 30 minutes of reading/research and note taking
- Day 2: 30 minutes of reading/research and note taking

- Day 3: Sketch out a rough outline of the essay
- Day 4: Go to the library/use the internet to identify any additional source material and research needed
- Day 5: Write the conclusions
- Day 6: Write the first argument...

You get the picture. By focusing only on the task immediately at hand, the entire thing isn't so daunting, AND you get a sense of progress and achievement on a regular basis. Plus, the bonus benefit is that your brain can be working away in the background – you'll find that when it actually comes time to sit down and write, the words flow much more readily.

So, when you suspect that the cause of your procrastination is what I like to call "Blank Page Syndrome" the first task is simply to break the process down into its individual stages or phases, and then do the first one. Then the second. Until eventually its all complete without the overwhelm.

Fear Of Rejection And/Or Failure

Another common cause of procrastination is fear of rejection.

At the moment of writing this, I'm nearing completion of the first draft of this book. And I noticed this week that I haven't been nearly as motivated to write as I normally am. It's been a bit like swimming in treacle.

Initially, I thought I was tired and just needed a bit of time – a couple of days – to get some extra sleep and get back on top of things. But then I realised that once the first draft is complete, not only am I going to need to start working on revisions, but I'm a whole lot closer to *showing this to somebody else*. While it's an incomplete bunch of words in my computer, nobody cares. I feel like I've created something, but nobody needs to know.

But what if my test readers don't like it? What if my editor doesn't like it? What if I don't like it?

What if you don't like it?

Fear of rejection is intrinsic to being human. But it doesn't have to be.

The first thing to do is to see it for what it is. I'm worried that if you don't like it, you and the rest of my tribe will abandon me, and I'll be left to fend for myself…

Hang-on a minute. I mean, I like you and everything, but I've only known you for a few thousand words. It's not as if I'm depending on you for the survival of my family! I think we'll be OK even if you don't like it. I mean I really hope you do, because I don't want you saying bad things about me, or thinking I wasted your time or anything, but ultimately, I'll be OK.

Second, List the things that will happen if you are rejected.

Seriously, write them down on a piece of paper.

- You won't finish reading the book
- You won't recommend the book
- You might say something bad about the book on social media
- You might give me a one-star review at your favourite bookseller
- You might tell a friend not to buy the book…

Are any of these life-threatening? No.

Even if you're the New York Times book reviewer, you not liking my book is not the end of the world. I will survive. I may even learn something.

I'll be OK.

Third, recognise that everything good in the world came about because somebody overcame the fear of rejection or failure. You came about because your parents both overcame the fear of being rejected by the other. Great businesses are built when sales reps and entrepreneurs embrace failure and rejection as part of the cost of doing business. Everyone who has ever 'led' anybody or anything has grappled with the idea that they might turn around to find nobody following them.

You'll be OK. Don't let fear of rejection or failure stop you from making progress.

Laziness

We've covered this a bit already in this book, but it's worthy of restatement. Your brain is incredibly efficient at finding ways to conserve energy. And the best way to conserve energy is to do less. Or better still, do nothing. But let me put your mind at ease. You have access to more highly calorific food than anybody in the history of human kind. I'm not suggesting you break out the comfort food – far from it. I'm simply pointing out that this is irrational and unnecessary.

You only get one life. You are obliged to do the most you can with it. For your own legacy, for your family, and for the world.

Nigel will try and convince you something else is going on here, but it really isn't.

Get off the couch, get off social media, stop watching TV. Make it happen!

Fear Of Success

Believe it or not, many people – when they start getting close enough to the thing they've been striving for – start to worry about what happens when they achieve it. This is at the heart of personal investment.

You have been so focused on this thing, for so long now, that it has almost become part of who you are. It's part of your identity. It's how you introduce yourself at networking events and parties.

But here's the thing. Once you've achieved the thing, you'll be the person who achieved the thing. That's way more cool than the person trying to achieve the thing! Besides, I don't think you need to have any concerns… you'll find more things!

Final Thoughts On Procrastination

There are other reasons you might be procrastinating or delaying the next stage of your plan.

Nigel might be trying to convince you that you're neglecting something else you are responsible for. Like you might not be spending as much time with your family as you should. To overcome this, you need to make some very **deliberate** and **active** decisions to spend quality time with them. Not half-engaged time, but fully-engaged time. No cell phones, no laptops. Play a game. Go for a bike ride. Read a book together.

You may have concerns that the plan is no longer the *right* plan. The nature of the goals you've set means that there isn't likely to be one right answer for how to get there. In fact there are probably many alternative pathways. Try not to spend too much time worrying about the path not travelled. Or if you're right, and you do need to recalibrate, don't muck around. Do it quickly before the sunk costs get any higher.

You may have concerns that you're not up to the task. Well you may be right. But guess what. That's what other people are for. Somebody will be. You just have to find them, and recruit them. Add that to your plan and move on.

23. Persistence – Overcoming People's Resistance

*"The resistance that you fight physically in the gym
and the resistance that you fight in life can only build
a strong character."* Arnold Schwarzenegger

Resistance from *other* people tends to come in a slightly greater variety of forms. Persistence is the basic answer to virtually all of them, but it is worth unpicking this a bit more.

People become invested in things they've spent time or energy on. The more time and energy they've invested, as a general rule, the more invested they are likely to be.

This doesn't hold true for absolutely everyone, but it's a useful rule of thumb.

I mean, think about it. If you built something, you care about it more. If you spent a lot of time researching the perfect sofa, you'll love it much more than if you just popped into your local sofa shop and picked the first one you saw. The longer you live in a house, the harder it is to move. This simple truth lies behind Ikea's success… if you spent three hours sprawled on the floor trying to read the instructions for the new dresser you bought, you're going to be pretty proud of it once it's built!

We upgraded our car recently. There was nothing particularly wrong with the old one, but it wasn't really big enough, and our son is getting bigger (also known as taller!) and now has a bike and numerous other activities that need car space. So we took possession of the new car before we sold the old one, and as we were preparing to sell the old car, both my husband and I became very sentimental about it. It's the car that we went to hospital in when I went into labour. It is the car we brought our son home from the hospital in. It is the first car we owned... I think you get the picture.

The longer you've had something or done something, the more memories and experiences you will associate with that thing. The harder it is to let it go. Sometimes this happens even with things that annoy us or that we complain about.

I have made changes to processes and systems at work on the basis of information (and complaints) from my team, only to realise they either didn't really expect me to do anything about it, or they weren't being completely honest with themselves about their true feelings about that process. Sometimes 'new' is scarier than old and annoying.

Making changes to things also threatens people's sense of security.

Let's say, for just a minute that the answer to my big curly problem – ridding the country of abuse and violence against children – involved getting rid of the current model of state-funded social workers that go into homes once enough indicators suggest there is an issue (say calls from concerned neighbours, or domestic violence police call-outs), and instead, replace them with community educators, whose role was to teach emotional resilience, coping skills and communication skills to expecting parents and their wider family unit.

Now even if I made it really clear that every existing social worker would be trained and supported to become one of these new community educators, and even if they all were guaranteed to retain their employment, and even if you offered them a pay rise and a better set of terms and conditions, there would be a significant number who would be unhappy with the idea. What I'm saying is, even if you resolve all the potential obvious causes of fear or uncertainty, you still haven't resolved the emotional connection and investment in the status quo.

Some of them will know they found the training for becoming a social worker really difficult, and not want to go through that process again, no matter how much support you provide.

Some of them will be passionate social workers and really believe in the power of a compassionate social worker to make a meaningful difference in the lives of young people. And they'd be right… they would have a career's worth of experience and evidence to back it up – compared with no evidence that this new-fangled thing will work.

Some of them will have a tendency towards pessimism, and think the 'Pollyanna-ish' idea that you can change people's underlying behaviour through education is a fool's game, and then you'll still need social workers, so why change it.

I guess what I'm trying to say is, even if your plan and execution are flawless – from concept through to implementation – there will still be people who don't think it's a good idea and will resist what you are proposing.

So what can you do about it?

Persist.

Try new approaches, but…

Persist.

Get up tomorrow and try again.

Remind yourself why you're doing this.

Search inside and remind yourself of whose interests you have at heart. Is it your own? No? Then…

Persist.

If the thing you are striving for is big enough and worthy enough, you are guaranteed to encounter resistance. What rhymes with resist?

Persist!

If the thing you are striving for was easy to solve, somebody else would have done it already.

Persist.

If you meet an impenetrable brick wall… try and find another way. A way over. A way under. A way around. Look for a door. Or even a window.

Don't give up. Remember the outcome you're seeking. Is it worthwhile? Then keep going.

What will the world be like if you succeed? Focus on that.

Keep telling your story. Keep finding new ways to tell the story. You might find a way of telling the story that resonates with someone… and they drop their resistance.

Try many different styles of approach. Take a long run-up. Use a springboard. At least metaphorically speaking.

Seek advice from other people. Don't forget this one. It's really important. There will be someone out there who can help you break through. Try and imagine what this looks like for the people who are resisting your actions. By understanding their perspective, you'll be better equipped to overcome it.

Try not to get into siege mentality though. This is important. When you're pushing, pushing, pushing, all day, every day for weeks on end, it can be easy to slip into frustration – or even anger. Your mindfulness practice should see you right here, but don't become frustrated, because it tends to reduce the quality of your thinking and it can cloud your judgment. Too many of the wrong approaches can lead to an increase in resistance – and you don't want that!

If you sense you are becoming frustrated, take a pause. Focus on another aspect of the plan for a few days. Get some 'emotional' distance. Regroup. Recharge.

But don't give up.

If it matters – it's worth some discomfort.

So…

Persist.

24. Measure Your Results

"I have been struck again and again by how important measurement is to improving the human condition." Bill Gates

Now I have to confess, this section is the most daunting for me.

I'm going to make a sweeping generalisation and say that, as a rule, New Zealanders are more data-averse than many other populations. I've worked in organisations that should be very data savvy, and I've often found that the people doing the groundbreaking analytics aren't Kiwis. They're expatriates from the United Kingdom, or the United States, or Australia. This is not just my perception. I've discussed it with a lot of people in a lot of different contexts, and – while they all note exceptions – there is general agreement.

In fact in Australia I had the absolutely phenomenal privilege of working with a brilliant guy from Sierra Leone who was able to build a costing model of the entire Australian social welfare support system in Excel, using probabilities and statistical data rather than actual population data.

It was a joy to behold. It accurately predicted the cost of changes to entitlements and benefits based on policy descriptions. It was awesome. And while I could understand how it worked, and I was able to work with the team to use the model, I could never have built it. Or maybe I could have – I'm OK with spreadsheets and I understand numbers, but I would never have had the *idea* to build it. I don't get excited about random numbers enough to ask "how could I use this data to tell me a story". Present me with data and I can interpret it and understand it.

None of this though means that I can escape including a section on metrics and measurement in a book about creating change and setting massive goals. Measuring results is important for a few reasons.

First, your personal sense of fulfilment is going to come from the sense of progress you have along the journey – not necessarily in reaching your destination. Not least of all because part way through the journey you may realise that the destination you had in mind isn't quite the right one. Without a sense of progress, this could seem like failure. But it almost certainly isn't, and often leads to a much better outcome overall.

Second, when the going gets tough, and it will, you need to be able to look back at how far you've come. This is very hard to do in any quantifiable way without some metrics that show progress or growth. Remember that Nigel will be busily normalising your progress as the new status quo. Frequently. This helps him be comfortable. "Oh", he says, "this is how things have always been". If you feel stuck, and you look back and he says "nah, this is how it always was" you will give up. You need to know it's been worth it so far.

Third, even if you can see exactly where you are going and you *feel* why you are doing it with every fibre of your being, there will be people around you who need you to show them the evidence. In more or less detail than you are naturally inclined to create. Some will want to know exactly how many steps there are from here to there. Others will want to know how what you are doing impacts on one or two key metrics that *they* care about.

Fourth, your toughest sceptics will interpret a lack of data as evidence that you don't know what you're doing, and may use it to undermine you.

All this is to say you need to think about how you will measure what you are trying to do, and how you will know whether you are on the right track.

Now if you think right back to the section we covered on SMARTER goals. You'll remember that the M stands for Measurable.

You will have done some thinking about measuring progress at that time. But now's a good point to double check it. Particularly with all the new information and knowledge you now have about what to expect along the way.

Now I do have some advice about what works for me. But I'd like you to note that this is probably a minimum-necessary approach (I'm a Kiwi after all). So please feel free to elaborate and exceed what I set out here... Within reason. Remember Nigel? He loves this stuff... It's like research. It's another way to avoid actually doing anything uncomfortable. I mean designing how you'll measure 'impact' isn't actually 'impact'. Right?

Qualitative And Quantitative

First, let's make a distinction between two primary types of measurement. Qualitative and quantitative.

In its simplest form, qualitative measurement usually looks more like a story or an anecdote. Or it describes the quality of something. It's very hard to measure, for example, the actual improvement in the quality of a service in any other way than stories about satisfied customers, or service reps reporting that things seem to be better.

Quantitative on the other hand, means something that can be counted or measured. If you are relying on qualitative metrics heavily for what you are doing, try and see if there are ways that they can be 'backed up' by qualitative metrics. For example, "not only are we receiving anecdotal feedback that people are finding our service easier to use, but we are experiencing a 20% reduction in call volumes to our help desk".

In an ideal world, you have both. Reliance on either without the other will lead to a less compelling narrative. It's hard to get emotional about data, but illustrate it with a story or two and you're in a whole other ball game.

Inputs, Outputs And Outcomes

Second, we need to understand what we are actually going to measure.

If you think of your activity as a 'system' for producing the goal you're seeking, there are three distinct points in the system that can be measured: what you put into it – your effort, energy, time and money; what comes out the end of the system – meetings, products, connections, relationships; and what impact those things have in the world – awareness, behaviour change, and a cascade of social good that might come from that.

You'll notice that the further through the 'system' you move, the less direct control you have over the thing that is being measured.

Let's look at a really simple example. Fundraising.

There are a bunch of things you need to do to raise funds – calling potential funders, meeting with them, publishing ads, blog posts and events that 'advertise' the fact you're seeking funds. These can all be counted: time spent, meetings held, people spoken to, dollars spent on promotion. These are all examples of inputs. It's what you 'put in'. These lend themselves very nicely to quantitative measurement, but it's a good idea to try and build in some qualitative measures too, otherwise you might make 16 calls when you're having a really bad day – and even if you're reading from a script, it'll be hard to convert the calls into qualified meetings. So you could set a target to measure the number of high-energy query calls. Or the proportion of cold calls, to follow-up calls.

Then there are some things that are produced as a consequence of the inputs you provide. Social shares and engagement with your cause is one of these. You've created and published a post or ad, and there's a consequence to that. At this stage you can't tell whether the engagement is good or bad – page views on a website doesn't tell you whether people were sympathetic to your message or not. In fact even bounce-rate and time spent on page don't tell you very much.

Depending on your overall goal, you may decide that the quantity of funds raised is actually an output – because you're raising funds for a purpose, so the amount of funds raised isn't actually the outcome you're seeking. This will depend on what your goal is.

Finally there is the change created by the inputs and the outputs. If you raise the target level of funds and then you donate that money to a worthy cause, that might be the outcome you were seeking. However, you may go one step further, and seek to measure the actual change created by the funds donated. Again, this can get tricky to distinguish between outputs and outcomes. Most charities are great at telling you exactly how they spent the money they've received – but it can be harder to discern the impact that money has had. For example, a reduction in child mortality might be an outcome of a charity investing in water purification and sanitation infrastructure.

One of the characteristics of outcomes (which usually means you're on the right track) is that it can start to get messy. It can be really hard to tell whether you are entirely responsible for the outcome or not. Usually, you aren't. In our example, there might be two other charities doing work in the same place – there might be one providing medical services, and another educating new mums about the health and wellbeing of their new babies… all three charities will be impacting (or should be impacting) on the outcome of child mortality – and it will be virtually impossible to prove how much was contributed by each.

Which is actually quite nice, because it suggests all three should work together rather than competing for funds or kudos!

At the end of the day, though, you must include the outcome you're aiming for – this is aligned with your why and your inspiration. If you focus just on what you control and what's easy to measure, you'll never really know if you made any difference at all

– you'll just know you put in a whole lot of effort and did some stuff. That's not very fulfilling or inspiring!

Bringing It All Together...

Don't worry, I'm not going to leave you hanging there. The last step in this phase is to draw these pieces together in a simple but relatively comprehensive framework[*].

This is commonly referred to as 'intervention logic'. It's a diagrammatical representation of what you're aiming to achieve, and how you're proposing to do it, with the various measurement points along the way. You'll probably find that you need to include some 'assumption statements' to link the outcomes and the outputs together in a logical way.

Start with the end in mind – the outcome you're seeking. I'd be willing to bet that this is almost word for word your big hairy goal – though you may need to break it down a bit. Next to each component, put the metric you'll use. It might be somebody else's job to collect this data – for example it could be a publicly reported data set, like national statistics.

Leave a decent sized gap, then below that, list the things you're going to 'produce'. The outputs. Next to each, include how many, costs et cetera – whatever metrics are relevant here.

Now using the gap you created between the two, show how the outputs are linked to the outcomes, including any assumptions you need to make to create this 'logic leap'. You may even find it helpful

---

[*] I've included a worksheet for doing this on my website www.RebeccaElvy.com/BookResources

to include your knowledge about other 'players' contributing to this outcome, and your assumptions about what they are doing.

Again, leave another gap, then put the inputs you'll make and the metrics you'll collect. Then use the gap to show how the inputs become outputs. This should be slightly easier than above, because you have more control over this part of the system.

So a simple worked (fictional) example might look like this:

- Outcome: Reduction in infant and child mortality caused by unsafe drinking water in x-village from 6.7% to 3.5% within five years. Data collected by the World Health Organisation and published annually on their website
- Intervention Logic: Building wells increases the availability of safe drinking water, and enables access to clean water for cooking and cleaning implements used to feed young children. It also reduces instances of waterborne diseases like dysentery, cholera and... (et cetera). Doctors without Borders are also operating in x-village, so working with them to ensure the placement of the wells is in line with their knowledge about where they are likely to have the most impact, would be beneficial
- Outputs: Five wells built each year for five years. On the ground, work with the community to ensure they understand the importance of sanitation and safe drinking water (so they don't inadvertently pollute

their wells or other unanticipated consequences). Each well costs $4,500 and the community work is undertaken by trained volunteers

- Intervention Logic: The volunteers are able to communicate effectively with the people in the community, and are able to engage directly with Doctors without Borders volunteers effectively

- Inputs: $ for wells, $ for flights and support for volunteers, $ for advertising for volunteers and donors, education programme to deliver to volunteers... et cetera

This should give you the rough idea.

Like everything in this book, I guarantee you that if you do this, you'll get a better outcome – but it almost certainly won't be exactly the outcome you expected. As you go, you'll learn whether your assumptions were correct, or some things will cost more or take longer. But that is exactly the point. You'll use what you record in this intervention logic map to assess your progress and tell that story to others. If you like, it's the 'potted' version of your hypothesis. If you aren't clear about what you expect to happen, you'll never know whether it did or not.

The other benefit is that it helps you troubleshoot. If you're halfway through your project, and you've achieved everything you intended to, in the area of inputs and outputs, but the infant and child mortality rates aren't budging, you know you need to dig into the assumptions you made between your outputs and the outcome you're seeking. Were you just overly ambitious? Is there a communication problem between the people who live in the village and your volunteers? Is the water available from the wells actually meeting the 'safe' standards you expected?

This is the nitty-gritty bit – and it can be really hard, but I promise it's worth it. And done well, not only will it be of great solace to you when you're having a down day, but it can also help put the writing on the wall if your approach is flawed *before* you've completely invested everything you intended.

Furthermore, it's a great way to persuade your greatest critics that you're onto something they should get behind!

Part Seven: Insight 🦋

25. Introducing Insight

"There is nothing so terrible as activity without insight." Johann Wolfgang von Goethe

At this point in your process, you'll be kicking some serious backside. You're inspired, you have intent, you're having an impact...

But how do you know if it's working? Are you on the right track?

Nigel keeps piping up in that niggly way of his to suggest that it's not going to work... Suggesting that you haven't got what it takes... Suggesting that you aren't qualified... And while you've become far more adept at telling him to be quiet and mind his own business, part of what he has to say gets through...

I mean it's hard work, right? There aren't any clear signposts to show you which way to go… What if it doesn't work? Was it all a waste of time? Should you just leave it to the big boys and stop pretending you're bigger and more capable than you are…

Oooh, see how he does that! Nigel is slick… he gets under your skin and then tries to start sounding like he's *you* again! But he's not. Not in any practical or realistic way. He's the prehistoric you, worried about sabre-tooth tigers and where your next meal is coming from. He's trying to look out for you – he doesn't want you to waste your energy or resources – he wants to keep you 'safe'. He simply lacks the knowledge and understanding – the practical tools – to actually be of use to you.

As an aside – wouldn't it be amazing if you could upgrade Nigel to actually know what was genuinely risky!

Anyway, in this section we'll look at a few non-Nigel ways to figure out whether you are on track and to gain the *genuine* insights you need to increase your chances of success.

I've positioned this as an annual review – but to be honest, it's worth doing more frequently. Quarterly is ideal.

Just don't wait more than a year…

26. Feedback Loops

"I think it's very important to have a feedback loop, where you're constantly thinking about what you've done and how you could be doing it better." Elon Musk

Now I touched on this very briefly in the introduction, but I'm about to share with you the absolute most obvious thing in the whole world that hardly anyone knows about. It tends to emerge more frequently in business literature, but in all honesty, the more we can increase its profile amongst the general public as a good way of doing things, the better!

It's called a feedback loop.

Now I said it's obvious, and it is... when you see it you'll go "well duh". And I don't mind you saying that. I won't be upset (shh, Nigel – this isn't about you).

Within academic circles, it's very closely aligned with scientific method... so if you're trained as a scientist, you may want to skip this section. Although, I'm not sure whether you've thought deeply about how to apply it to your day-to-day life. Anyway, this is how it should work – and then I'll explain where it usually falls down. For most people at least – but quite a few companies and NGOs as well.

You have a problem. Big – small – medium-sized, doesn't matter.

You ponder it for a while, and then you think you might have a way to solve the problem. So you do that. Then you take a look to see if it worked. Then based on what you see, you either keep doing what you are doing (because it's working) or you change it slightly to make improvements (because it could be better) or you go back to the drawing board, because it hasn't worked at all... rinse and repeat.

Makes sense, right?

Design... implement... evaluate... refine... and so on around the loop, again, and again, and again, until you've had the desired impact.

What could possibly go wrong?

Well, too often, we aren't very explicit that this is what we're doing. So we kind of muddle along, and it works or it doesn't, and we're not really clear about what happened. Or we try three different approaches at the same time, but we can't tell which one is working and which ones aren't. Or we solve the problem remarkably well, but we're not really sure why it worked so we can't easily replicate it if a similar situation arises again in the future.

Now we'll spend a little more time on this shortly, but this book is a giant feedback loop...Get inspired, get intentional, create an impact, gain insight... and do it all over again.

That's not an accident. It works because it's simple. It works because its effective. It works because it systematically removes the guesswork from experimenting with human solutions to human problems in the real world which, as we all know, is messy and frequently unpredictable.

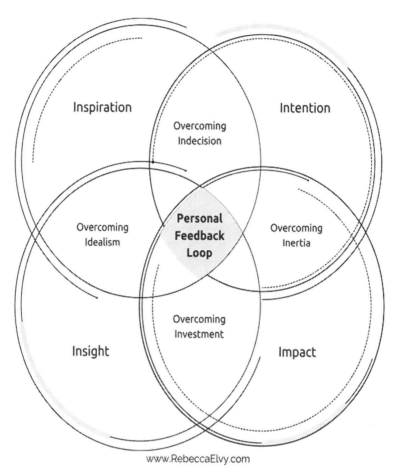

Inspiration

Intention

Overcoming
Indecision

Overcoming
Idealism

**Personal
Feedback
Loop**

Overcoming
Inertia

Overcoming
Investment

Insight

Impact

www.RebeccaElvy.com

The other way that our 'un-intended' feedback loops go wrong is because we haven't designed the experiment well. We can't tell what actions had what impacts.

But it fails most often because by the time we get to the end (insight and evaluation) we're exhausted and we forget/don't bother to close the loop. We lose interest. It either worked or it didn't. What difference does it make to do a post-mortem now? How many times have you been on a project team where all the energy and enthusiasm gets spent on the planning and the implementation (and even the data collection and reporting) and then nobody bothers with the project close-out meeting and report?

Partly this is because of our fear of failure. We don't like anybody questioning our competence – and we especially don't want to provide them with the ammunition for doing so! But it's usually relief. The project is done. We've finished... on to the next one. On to the next one. We're always more excited by novelty. By shiny new things. By new prospects. By new opportunities. New new new.

And while I have no problem with new – I'm just as guilty of this as the next person – our society would be better off if we properly extracted the lessons from our various separate activities and made them digestible to others.

Hardly anyone ever takes the time to look at what has been tried before. Have you ever noticed when a new manager comes into a workplace, they spend hardly any time 'exploring' the idea that much of what had happened before they arrived might have been worthwhile and effective?

No, wheel-reinvention is a national pastime. Where's Nigel on that! He should have something to say about that much wasted energy and effort! But no... he's quiet on this. Not sure why. Maybe he assumes he's more clever than everyone else who tried...

Anyway, the feedback loop is deceptively simple, but it's almost always ignored. Absorb it into your psyche. It's so simple you can't really forget it. Make the most of it.

Turn it into a fly-wheel, in the words of the brilliant Jim Collins, author of *Good to Great*, and avoid the doom-loop of constant reinvention with no progress in between.

27. Review Your Inspiration

Part of your process should be to revisit your inspiration. Why did you start this gig in the first place? What was your deep-seated, intrinsic "why"? Who is it for? What will be better for them if you succeed? What would the world be like if you achieved everything you had hoped you would?

Then ask yourself this question... Do you still care?

I say this not because I expect you've become so jaded as part of your process that you're ready to curl up in a ball and hide from the world for a few months (be careful – don't let Nigel hear that) but because sometimes, you discover that there's actually something more important. Something that does the first thing, but also more.

I might make some traction on reducing violence against children, and then realise that the real perpetrator is poverty... and I might realise I'm actually *more* inspired by the idea of tackling that. It might have even more positive benefits for society, or it might be better aligned with my natural areas of expertise, so I expect I could have more impact. It might be that the government has introduced policies that overlap with what you're doing, and you no longer need to play such an active role...

All of these things can mean that you get to the end of the process and are no longer quite so inspired by the thing you set out to achieve. If that is the case, it may well be time to move onto the next project... just don't do it before you complete your review process – extract every lesson and insight you can before you move on. Even if your next mission appears unrelated, there will be transferable lessons. Be curious.

Even if your area of inspiration *hasn't* changed, and you're still just as passionate about it as you were when you started, make sure you take some time to reflect on it. The world will have changed in the intervening period. You may find that there are new sources of relevant inspiration that make you even more determined. It might be time to update your vision board.

Keeping that inspiration front and centre is absolutely crucial to remaining motivated through the tough times… you know that now, you've been there. So don't short-change yourself on this re-connection. What was the gap you identified initially? Have you moved the needle on it? Or has the goalpost moved? If so, is the new goal just as inspiring? Does this get your socks rolling up and down? Are you leaping out of bed in the morning ready to tackle this exciting problem? Are you energised? Do you find it hard to think about other things?

Revisit the 'finding your why' section from the beginning of the book. Chances are, by this point, there are more people than you interested in the 'mission' you're on. Get them involved. Create a 'why' for the team. Discuss it. You might find you all have slightly different reasons for wanting to create change, but that they all dovetail into each other neatly. You might find your own inspiration increases because of *other people's* inspiration. That's great. It doesn't all have to be about you!

Take a look back and try and recall any moments through the process so far where the inspiration you created at the start didn't seem sufficient. Those long late nights. The rejections from backers or potential donors. The disinterest from other people you thought would care. Those are the long dark winters. Was your inspiration sufficient to help you keep going? Or did it waver? Did you nearly pack it in and give up? Or did it make your resolve stronger and more resolute? Can you anticipate any reason why it will be harder this time around?

Your answers to these questions should inform how much time you spend reconnecting with your why. Hopefully you do this daily on a small scale anyway, but if you need a complete revamp, that's OK.

Even if you've decided to move onto something new, this 'revisit' is important. Because there are lessons to be learnt about how much inspiration is necessary for the scale of the task. It isn't a strictly linear relationship, but it is correlated. So if you are tackling a bigger and more ambitious goal next, you'll use the insight you gain here to calibrate how much 'inspiration juice' you need to find in the initial stages of the new project.

Remain mindful. What causes you discomfort? What makes you angry? What makes you sad? Where can you see pain in the world? What gap needs to be closed? What hurt needs to be healed? That is where your heart is leading you. Go there. Do that.

And to hell with Nigel.

28. Reset Your Intent

Are you re-inspired? Great!

Let's get intentional about intent.

Create a time to look back over all the planning and preparation you did in setting your intent. The strategic thinking. The research. The SMARTER goals. Was it sufficient? How much of it did you use and refer to often? How much did you never go back to? How accurate were your strategic insights – did the future unfold more or less as you expected? Were you able to anticipate some of the likely points of contention and resistance? Also, the world has probably changed a bit. What developments in the external environment – politics, legislation, demographics, the economy – mean your expectations about what happens next might need a rethink?

Remember, at this stage in the process, you're gaining insights from what you *did* to inform what you'll *do*. So this isn't (yet) about re-diving into strategic thinking and forecasting, or research, or documenting your plans. It's about reviewing what you did to see whether it helped you. And more specifically, to get really clear about what did help you so that you can ensure you do that again or improve it for next time.

A note of caution though. Don't be too hasty to discard things that didn't seem useful. If your next goals are as ambitious as your last ones, you should be mindful that you will have internalised a lot of what you learned through those processes. Just because you didn't refer to one of the documents you created – say your research outline – at all during the process doesn't mean it wasn't supporting and enhancing your decision-making on a day-to-day basis just by sitting in the back of your mind.

What further research did you need to undertake along the way? Was your initial research mostly in the right areas? Were you able to identify the things you *needed* to know more about from the things that Nigel *wanted* you to get distracted by?

What about your planning processes. Did you find your goal was articulated sufficiently well to be useful to you as you made your way through what I'm *sure* was a rather messy minefield of competing priorities and red herrings? Could you clearly illuminate the next couple of steps so that you could take action? Or did you struggle with the idea that you needed to map out the whole journey before you could start?

How did you go with deadlines? Were you too ambitious? Downright unrealistic? Or about right? What did you learn about your own capacity and capability to deliver along the way? Were you pleasantly surprised? Did you sometimes feel you'd let yourself down? (Be quiet Nigel – this isn't about you.)

Are you actually a perfectionist? That's tricky. Nothing is ever perfect. Perfectionism can be debilitating. It's also a great place for Nigel to hide. Remember you can always refine more later, but almost always, done is better than perfect.

How good are you at specifying measures and targets? Did you pick things to measure that provided genuine insight into your progress? Were they useful to you in guiding decision-making and action steps along the way? If not, what would you need to change next time? More of them? Less of them? Better systems for measuring things? Better systems for capturing the *insights* from that measurement?

It's not uncommon, when you're tackling something really big – system-level change – to find that you are awash with data but bereft of insight. Don't assume that just because you can count something, that it is useful to do so. Likewise, just because something is incredibly hard to count, doesn't mean you can't find a way. And in fact, that it might be the only thing worth counting.

Now it might seem a bit counter-intuitive to spend time assessing how you planned to do this – what your intent was – from the outset. Especially if the project is still a work in progress. But I promise you this, there is never a better time to refresh and recommit to your plan than right now. You will find something that had slipped off the radar, that needs to be picked up. You will find something that you never intended to spend any time on at all, but actually has ended up absorbing a significant proportion of your effort. If you find this, the question is, should it have been in your plan – in which case, add it in now – or should you stop doing it because it's a distraction from the main game? You will find something that has been bubbling away alright, but when you revisit it, you realise it needs a major reboot. You will find something that you dismissed earlier because you didn't have the skills or connections, that you now do. Pick it up and dust it off.

There are, of course, bound to be some things that are ticking along exactly as you expected them to do. That's great feedback too! It means your planning skills, and your research and your strategic thinking, were sound and on track. Don't let this fool you though –

these are partly about your capability and attention to detail – and partly about luck. Getting it right once has only limited predictive value for getting it right again.

Clarifying and documenting your intent isn't just a one-off thing. Remember you are only ever planning out the next few steps, so hopefully you've been reminding yourself regularly to pause, reflect and recommit by setting the next few. And the next few.

Keep it up. You're doing fine.

29. Refresh Your Impact

Have you re-committed to your intended goal? Awesome – let's talk about impact and what insights it offers us.

So what did you actually achieve?

I'm serious. That's not a facetious question. What changed as a result of all your effort, and energy, and enthusiasm?

Is the world a better place? Is your community better off? Are you a better, kinder, more compassionate human being? Have you gained new skills and connections, that will enable you to achieve even more in the coming year than you did this year? Are you happy with what you've accomplished? Are the people who matter happy with what has been accomplished? Are the results more or less what you expected?

If not, in what areas are they different? Is it things that you can control? Or things that are impacted by others. What insights can you gain from this? Should you be doing something differently? Do you need to reach out and work with some different people or organisations? Can you approach the issue from a different angle to gain more traction?

Did the level of effort expended bear any correlation to the results achieved? If they didn't, do you care? You might not. You might be so inspired to resolve this problem – to close this gap – that any movement of the needle, no matter how small, is worth the effort.

Alternatively, you might be inspired now to try a different tack. Can you recruit more assistance from other people or organisations? Can you gain backing or funding from a new source? Are there any new players in this area that weren't around when you started, that might be interested in partnering with you?

Is there some form of disruption – digital or otherwise – going on in your sector? Can you see emerging evidence of something dramatic happening in the not-too-distant future? What does that mean for how much ground you've covered so far? Can you expect the same effort to garner the same results next year? Or will it get harder... or easier?

Are you the disruption?

Could you be?

How could you 10x your impact? How could you 10x your impact tomorrow?

I know these questions are uncomfortable. But sit with them.

Pick a couple. Ponder them deeply.

Journal about it.

Meditate on it.

Ask your brain and it will try and answer. Ask it often, and your brain will believe it's a question you care about. It will go out of its way to try and find you an answer. This is the heart of creativity. Trying to solve a problem for which there previously was no answer. You cannot Google it. You cannot research it.

You must create something new.

This is how you achieve impact.

Part Eight: Overcoming Idealism ✦

30. Introducing Idealism

"Many people think of perfectionism as striving to be your best, but it is not about self-improvement; it's about earning approval and acceptance." Brené Brown

While it is true that many of the best ideas are inherently simple and elegant, they don't start that way. Ideation – the act of creating ideas – is inherently messy. It's convoluted and sloppy and unreliable. It creates tension and unease. But throughout our daily lives we see examples, time and time again, of slick, polished, expertly marketed projects that appear effortlessly perfect. The iPod, then the iPhone. Products designed by Dyson. Packaging for cosmetics.

The beautifully packaged and complete products that we consume and interact with on a daily basis lull us into the misapprehension that great products *start out great*. They don't.

I know it's a cliché, but how many lightbulbs did Edison have to invent before he got it right? He changed the world though.

You see the end result. After the years of research and development, after the design team has had its way with it. After the marketing team has had its way with it. After the product testers and focus groups are finished.

And even with all this investment, how many products do you think are launched and fail every year?

On the positive side, with the advent of eCommerce and self-publishing and crowd-funding, it's also possible to see products that are less polished. Perhaps our ideas about ideas will become a little more realistic in the near future!

The point here though is this. Even if you don't consider yourself to be a perfectionist, I guarantee there is a part of you that wants to be 'right' straight away. To not have to fail. To not have to go back to the drawing board. Multiple times.

To nail it.

To be brilliant without practicing.

The odds aren't great though.

You probably need to get a bit comfy with failure. Make it your friend. Make it another sign of progress. Make it evidence that you're trying.

So let's take a look at a few things you can do to overcome your idealism.

31. Beating Perfectionism

Meditation

Now if you've learned anything at all about me in the course of reading this book, it's that I'm an advocate of meditation for solving many of life's greatest challenges, and overcoming idealism is no exception to the rule.

So why do I think meditation can help you in this particular instance? Because it enables you to be aware of your thoughts. In that moment when you're asking whether it's good enough yet, it enables you to reflect on the immediate "no, not yet" and ask a few more questions.

In my own experience, by the time I ask "is it done yet?" I'm already well inside the territory of diminishing returns. In other words, the additional effort is no longer delivering the same value as the effort that went before it. This is kind of like when you're pushing really hard to meet a deadline, and it's nearly 2.00 am, and you start getting slower, and less productive, and less effective... the brain slows down, your faculties diminish. The same thing can happen the longer you spend on a project or task. Not all the time you spend on it is equally good...

Yet how many times have you pushed on, not realising this was the case, only to realise that the 'finished' product was riddled with errors? Or the thing you were stuck on the night before took about 30 seconds with the benefit of a (partial) night's sleep and a cup of coffee?

Mindfulness allows you the best possible chance of recognising that point at which your time-to-value ratio plateaus and starts heading in the wrong direction... and mindfulness comes from meditation.

Pareto Principle

Also known as the 80-20 rule, this refers to the uncanny frequency with which the ratio between these two numbers shows up in our everyday lives... That 20% of your clients deliver 80% of your revenue. That 20% of your clients generate 80% of your headaches. And perhaps most relevant here, that 20% of your effort generates 80% of your impact.

Embrace this apparently naturally occurring mathematical relationship. Make friends with it. Get to know it well.

Accept that 80% perfect is probably good enough – and that's about the point when diminishing returns set in. You can always come back to the other 20% later if it really does turn out it was important!

Convert Goals Into Guides

For most people, the more concrete and specific a goal is, the better. Otherwise it is possible to hide within the vagary and the 'almost-ness' of it all. And for some people, ambiguity is a source of procrastination and paralysis. (Nigel loves ambiguity by the way... it's the perfect time for him to sow the seeds of doubt... because how can you prove him wrong!)

But for those people for whom perfectionism and idealistic tendencies are actually the stumbling block, the prospect of not delivering exactly to the very polished and perfect plan is overwhelmingly devastating. If this sounds like you, try using the word 'guide' instead of 'goal'.

I wish I was a Formula One driver. It's one of those 'if I was just starting out again I'd have done a few things differently' moments. I love the precision of it. The exacting standards. The knife-edge upon which the drivers balance every time they take to the track. Pushing hard enough to extract every ounce of performance from the car, but not so hard as to end up in the wall. It's beautiful. And it's a lot safer than it used to be.

But one of the things that always intrigued me lies in advice that drivers just starting their career in the other kinds of cars (like go-karts for instance) get when it's obvious you're going to crash. Look at where you want to go, not where you are going. If you think you might hit the wall, focus out on the track where you want to be.

During an interview with SUCCESS magazine, world champion racing driver Mario Andretti was asked for his number one tip for success in race car driving. He said, "Don't look at the wall. Your car goes where your eyes go."

Because what you focus on, is what you get. When you set goals, you focus on them. And you are far more likely to achieve them than if you didn't set them at all. But the reality is, sometimes the goals are not attainable. Or at least not under the current conditions.

Calling them guides instead of goals is a bit like widening the track ever so slightly. It doesn't mean you can't hit the wall, but you've got a bit more leeway. It also doesn't prevent you from finding the sweet spot and following the exact perfect racing line…

you can still achieve the goal. You can just get there with a little less anxiety and pressure. You're less likely to get mesmerised by the wall…

Celebrate Success… Often

When our goals are lofty and we have a tendency toward idealism, we tend to say 'but we're not there yet' a bit too often. We stay focused on the gap between where we are right now and where we *ought* to be, and don't spend enough time thinking about the distance we've already come.

So take time to stop and smell the roses. Celebrate your achievements. They are many. And they are frequent. It doesn't have to mean unfurling a 'mission accomplished' banner at the end of the first week. It might just be taking a moment to smile and think about what you achieved today.

It doesn't mean gloating. It doesn't mean lowering your standards. It just means recognising explicitly that every journey is made up of lots of small incremental steps, and that every single one of those steps is taking you just a little bit closer to where you are aiming to be.

Remember that your sense of achievement and fulfilment comes from the progress you make and the extent to which you personally grow to achieve it. It doesn't come from arriving at the destination exactly on time and on budget.

Conclusion 🦋

So no matter what you set out to do, you now have the tools to do it.

Whether it is earth-shatteringly mind-blowingly enormous or comfortably modest local impact. Whether it is about economic or social good. Whether it's about profit and commercial drivers or ridding the world of unconscious bias and racism. There is no such thing as an unworthy goal if the inspiration behind it is empowering, if the intent is good and the impact is... well... impactful.

The world faces many problems. Yes a few of them are pretty big. But we've solved big problems before. Daunting? Yes. Impossible? No.

Equally though, we face numerous smaller problems in our own backyards. From civic responsibility, to how effectively your local school is performing for the kids who attend.

Can you pause for a minute and imagine a world where everybody... OK maybe 80% of everybody... got up each morning and asked "what can I do today that would make a difference"? That would make the world an incrementally better place than it is right now?" It's hard to see how this wouldn't make a difference. Even if every contribution on its own was infinitesimal.

Just imagine if every person picked up one piece of rubbish tomorrow. Or if every one of those 'better than average' drivers indicated correctly. Or if every teacher found one way to make a difference for one child. Or if every social worker staked their career on a slightly riskier call in favour of the child instead of the rules. Or if every corporate CEO made a commitment towards sustainable energy consumption. Or if every parent made a little more effort to be present for their kids tomorrow… It's hard not to believe that the accumulation of all of these small gestures wouldn't have some sort of impact.

From a polluted stream to graffiti on public buildings. They are all problems to the person inspired to resolve them. And if that someone is you, then I take off my hat to you, and I say, I hope that my contribution has helped.

Because at the end of the day, reading this book can only take you so far.

It can inspire a little, and it can give you some tools and systems to help you. But it cannot create your intent. And it cannot deliver the impact you seek.

That is up to you.

You have the power within you to do something. You have the skills and knowledge. The connections and insights. You have the energy and the passion and the drive. And now you have the system to put it to use.

The world needs your leadership. There are plenty of ways you can make a meaningful contribution.

This is mine.

What is yours?

"And will you succeed? Yes, you will indeed. 98 and 3/4 percent guaranteed. Kid? You'll move mountains." Dr. Seuss – Oh! The Places you'll Go!

Acknowledgments ❧

This book would not have been possible without the phenomenal support, first and foremost, of my beloved husband and best friend, Dale. His encouragement, critique, and practical help on sometimes a daily basis, cannot be understated – I am deeply in your debt.

To my Mum and Dad, for doing the best you could with the tools you had. And for having great parents of your own. To Ron and Mel, to Dave and Dawn, and to Jean. You have all played a huge role in my upbringing. Practical role models of the very best kind.

To those career mentors who helped me by creating connections and opportunities to test myself, to be exposed to things I did not believe I could do. And for believing in me.

To my academic mentors for challenging me to be rigorous and data driven.

Chris, my dear friend, for putting up with my regular updates and for paying such fastidious attention to editing the first draft.

Henrik, for your inspiration and encouragement, for your thorough comments and feedback, and for your conceptual engagement with the content and the broader mission. You have kept me going at times when I wondered what it all was for.

To Matthew and Jessee for reading so carefully the early draft. And to both of you for your encouragement and accountability!

To my scrappy book-launch team for providing input and ideas on a range of things from the final title, to the cover design, to helping spread the word to those who need to read it.

To Honiana, Sarah, Charlotte, Jamie, Jackie and Di. I endeavour to serve you all in the only way I know how. I hope I can live up to your expectations. Your sage counsel, good humour and a smile from time to time all went a long way.

To Robin and Dallas, our household is indebted to you both. Without you, none of us would be able to do the things we do. Grandparents like you make the modern family possible.

Finally, to my dear son Logan. From the moment I laid eyes on you the ground shifted beneath me. I would literally go to the ends of the earth and back for you. Thank you for helping me to learn what is possible, and for giving me a new appreciation for life and for the wonder of the world around us.

Bibliography 🦋

Ariely, Dan; *The (Honest) Truth About Hishonesty: How We Lie to Everyone – Especially Ourselves.* New York: Harper Perennial, 2012

Barends, Eric; Barbara Janssen & Cedric Velghe; "Rapid Evidence Assessment of the Research Literature on the Effect of Goal Setting on Workplace Performance", Technical Report, December 2016; CIPD, https://www.cipd.co.uk/Images/rapid-evidence-assessment-of-the-research-literature-on-the-effect-of-goal-setting-on-workplace-performance_tcm18-16903.pdf

Barton, Andy; "How to Run a Marathon in your Mind: 12 Tips for Winning the Mental Fight", The Guardian, 16 April 2015, https://www.theguardian.com/lifeandstyle/the-running-blog/2015/apr/16/how-to-run-a-marathon-12-tips-mental-fight

Carnegie, Dale; *How to Win Friends & Influence People.* New York: Simon & Schuster, 1936

Collins, Jim; *Good to Great: Why Some Companies Make the Leap and Others Don't.* New York: Harper Business, 2001

Covey, Stephen M. R.; *The Speed of Trust: The One Thing That Changes Everything.* New York: Free Press, 2006

Coyle, Geoff; *Practical Strategy: Structured Tools and Techniques.* Essex: Pearson Education Limited, 2004

De Bono, Edward; *Lateral Thinking: A Textbook of Creativity.* New York: Harper Perennial, 1970

Duckworth, Angela; *Grit: The Power of Passion and Perseverance.* New York: Scribner, 2016

Heath, Chip & Heath Dan; *The Power of Moments: Why Certain Experiences Have Extraordinary Impact.* New York: Simon & Schuster, 2017

Hill, Napoleon; *Think and Grow Rich (Revised and Expanded by Arthur R. Pell).* London: Vermilion, 2004

Hyatt, Michael; *Your Best Year Ever: A 5-Step Plan for Achieving Your Most Important Goals.* Grand Rapids: Baker Books, 2018

Keltner, Dachar; *The Power Paradox: How We Gain and Lose Influence.* New York: Penguin Books, 2016

Liedtka, Jeanne, Andrew King & Kevin Bennett; *Solving Problems with Design Thinking: Ten Stories of What Works.* New York: Columbia University Press, 2013

Mohr, Tara; *Playing Big: Practical Wisdom for Women Who Want to Speak Up, Create, and Lead.* New York: Avery, 2014

Robbins, Mel; *The 5 Second Rule: Transform Your Life, Work and Confidence with Everyday Courage.* A Savio Republic Book, 2017

Rubin, Gretchen; *The Four Tendencies: The Indispensable Personality Profiles That Reveal How to Make Your Life Better (and Other People's Lives Better, Too).* New York: Harmony Books, 2017

Schulz, Kathryn; *Being Wrong: Adventures in the Margin of Error.* New York: Ecco, 2010

Sinek, Simon; *Start With Why: How Great Leaders Inspire Everyone To Take Action.* London: Penguin Books, 2009

Sinek, Simon, David Mead & Peter Docker; *Find Your Why: A Practical Guide for Discovering Purpose for You and Your Team.* New York: Portfolio/Penguin, 2017

Thaler, Richard & Cass Sunstein; *Nudge: Improving Decisions About Health, Wealth, and Happiness.* New York: Penguin, 2008

Urban, Tim; "Neuralink and the Brain's Magical Future", Wait But Why, https://waitbutwhy.com/2017/04/neuralink.html

Vaden, Rory; *Procrastinate on Purpose: 5 Permissions to Multiply Your Time.* New York: Perigee, 2015

Wiseman, Richard; *The Luck Factor: The Scientific Study of the Lucky Mind.* New York: Hyperion, 2003

Zimbardo, Phillip & John Boyd; *The Time Paradox: Using the New Psychology of Time to Your Advantage.* London: Rider, 2008

Made in the USA
Middletown, DE
17 February 2022

61375056R00205